ISBN 978-1-332-19903-7
PIBN 10297145

This book is a reproduction of an important historical work. Forgotten Books uses
state-of-the-art technology to digitally reconstruct the work, preserving the original format
whilst repairing imperfections present in the aged copy. In rare cases, an imperfection in
the original, such as a blemish or missing page, may be replicated in our edition. We do,
however, repair the vast majority of imperfections successfully; any imperfections that
remain are intentionally left to preserve the state of such historical works.

Farmers, Mechanics, and Laborers need Protection—Capital can take care of itself.

SPEECH

OF

HON. WILLIAM D. KELLEY,

OF PENNSYLVANIA,

DELIVERED

IN THE HOUSE OF REPRESENTATIVES,

MARCH 25, 1870.

WASHINGTON:
F. & J. RIVES & GEO. A. BAILEY,
REPORTERS AND PRINTERS OF THE DEBATES OF CONGRESS.
1870.

Farmers, Mechanics, and Laborers need Protection—Capital can take care of itself.

The House being in the Committee of the Whole, and having under consideration the bill (H. R. No. 1068) to amend existing laws relating to the duties on imports, and for other purposes—

Mr. KELLEY said:

Mr. CHAIRMAN: I presume that gentlemen who have listened to the course of this debate expect me to apologize for having been born in Pennsylvania and adhering to my native State. From what has been said it seems that her people are regarded by free traders as a discreditable community, and she, in her corporate capacity, as an object of odium.

Sir, I am proud of dear old Pennsylvania, my native State. She was the first to adopt the Federal Constitution, and was in fact the key-stone of the Federal arch, holding together the young Union when it consisted of but thirteen States, and she is to-day preëminently the representative State of the Union. You cannot strike her so that her industries shall bleed without those of other States feeling it, and feeling it vitally. She has no cotton, or sugar, or rice fields; but apart from these she is identified with every interest represented upon this floor.

Gentlemen from the rocky coast of New England and the gentlemen who are here from the more fertile and hospitable shores of the Pacific, especially the gentlemen from the beautifully wooded shores of Puget sound, complain that their ship-yards are idle. Hers, alas! are also idle, although they are the yards in which were built the largest wooden ship the Government ever put afloat, and the largest sailing iron-clad it ever owned. She has her commerce and sympathizes with young San Francisco and our great commercial metropolis, New York. She was for long years the leading port of entry in the country. She still maintains a respectable direct commerce and imports, very largely through New York, for the same reasons that London does through Liverpool and Paris through Havre.

Are you interested in the production of fabrics, whether of silk, wool, flax, or cotton? If so her interests are identical with yours, for she employs as many spindles and looms as any New England State, and their productions are as various and valuable. Are your interests in the commerce upon the lakes? Then go with me to her beautiful city of Erie and behold how Pennsylvania sympathizes with all your interests there. Are your interests identified with the navigation of the Mississippi and seeking markets for your products at the mouth of that river and on the Gulf? I pray you to remember that two of the navigable sources of the American "Father of Waters" take their rise in the bosom of her mountains, and that for long decades her enterprising and industrious people have been plucking from her hills bituminous coal and floating it down that stream past the coal-fields of Ohio, Kentucky, Indiana, Illinois, Missouri, and other coal-bearing States, to meet that of England in the market of New Orleans and try to drive it thence. Gentlemen from the gold regions, where were the miners trained who first brought to light, with any measure of science and experience, the vast resources in gold and silver-bearing quartz of the Pacific slope? They went to you from the coal, iron, and zinc mines of Pennsylvania. There they had learned to sink the shaft, run the drift, handle the ore, and crush or smelt it. It was experience acquired in her mines that brought out the wealth of California almost as magically as we were taught in childhood to believe that Alladin's lamp could convert base articles into that precious metal.

Nor, sir, are the interests of Pennsylvania at variance with those of the great agricultural States? Before her Representatives in the two Houses of Congress had united their voices with those of gentlemen from the West to make magnificent land grants for the purpose of constructing railroads in different directions across the treeless but luxuriously fertile prairies,

Pennsylvania was first among the great agricultural States. And to-day her products of the field, the garden, the orchard, and the dairy equal in value those of any other State. Gentlemen from Ohio, notwithstanding the statement of the gentleman from Iowa, [Mr. ALLISON,] that you alone manufacture Scotch pig iron and suffer from its importation, as you alone have the black band ore from which it is made, is it not true that when Pennsylvania demands a tariff that will protect the wages of her laborers in the mine, quarry, and furnace, she does but defend the interest and rights of your laborers and those of every other iron-bearing State in the Union. Gentlemen from Virginia, Maryland, and North Carolina, Pennsylvania is denounced because she pleads for a duty on coal that will enable you to develop your magnificent tide-water coal fields in competition with Nova Scotia. The coal of your tide-water fields is far more available than that of the inland fields of Pennsylvania, which depend on railroads for transportation. On the banks of the James, the Dan, and a score of other navigable rivers, lie coalbeds to within a few hundred feet of which the vessels which are to carry the precious fuel away may come, and they lie nearer to the markets of New England than those of your colonial rivals at Nova Scotia; and when you were not here and Virginia and North Carolina were voiceless on this floor, I pleaded with the Thirty-Ninth Congress for the duty of $1 25 per ton in order that Virginia and North Carolina, soon to be reconstructed, should be able to produce fuel for New England better and cheaper than Nova Scotia does, and that it should be carried in New England built vessels, so that the thousands of people employed in producing and transporting it should constitute a market for the grain of the western farmer and the productions of American workshops. I might, Mr. Chairman, extend the illustration of the identity of the interests of Pennsylvania with those of the people of every other State, but will not detain the committee longer on that subject. In leaving it I however reiterate my assertion that you cannot strike a blow at her industries without the people of at least half a score of other States feeling it as keenly as she will. She asks no boon from Congress. Her people, whether they depend for subsistence upon their daily toil, or have been so fortunate as to have inherited or acquired capital, seek no special privileges from the Government. They demand that we shall legislate for the promotion of the equal welfare of all. They know that they must share the common fate, and that their prosperity depends upon that of their countrymen at large.

PROTECTION CHEAPENS COMMODITIES.

Mr. Chairman, many gentlemen have spoken since this bill was made a special order, and a great deal has been said upon the general subject of free trade and protection, and but little about the provisions embodied in the bill before the committee. I am probably expected to proceed at once to reply to the remarks of my colleague on the Committee of Ways and Means, [Mr. ALLISON,] who has just closed his remarks. But I may as well before proceeding to do so take a shot into the flock generally. The birds all have sung the same song. My colleague has gone more fully into the details of the bill than any of the others. But his statements are all in harmony with those of the several gentlemen who have given us the doctrines of the chief of the Bureau of Statistics, D. A. Wells, in their own admirable way. I propose to allude to some of their remarks.

The gentleman from New York [Mr. BROOKS] in opening the debate promised to mount a peddler's wagon and ride through the agricultural districts of the country exhibiting hoes, shovels, axes, chains, knives and forks, cottons, and woolens, and demonstrate to the people the unjust and enormous taxation imposed on them by the existing tariff. If the gentleman will redeem this promise, making candid statements of facts to the people I will contribute toward his expenses and pray for the success of his mission.

Mr. BROOKS, of New York. How much?

Mr. KELLEY. I will contribute 25 per cent., and what may be more effective, will try to make an arrangement by which the proprietors of Flagg's pain exterminator will give the gentleman a seat in their wagons while going through the country. By no other means could he so perfectly demonstrate the fact that duties which are really protective are never a tax, and that protection invariably cheapens commodities. So invariably is this true that protective America, France, and Germany are crowding free-trade England out of the markets of the world with the articles named by the gentleman, while purchasing the materials of which they are made from her and paying protective duties on every pound of it. This is not mere declamation. It is truth demonstrated by experience. The starving mechanics of England know it, and have at length succeeded in bringing it officially to the knowledge of Parliament. I have before me the report of a parliamentary commission which proves, that notwithstanding our duties on iron and steel, our knives and forks, horseshoe nails, &c., are crowding England out of general markets, that our hoes, shovels, and axes are bought by the people of all her colonies; and that our locks, sewing-machines, and other productions of iron and steel are underselling hers in the streets of London and Birmingham. There is the "report from the select committee on scientific instruction, together with the proceedings of the committee, minutes of evidence, and appendix," ordered by the House of Commons to be printed 15th July, 1868. It is a ponderous volume and replete with instruction.

I find on page 479 a paper handed in by Mr. Field, containing a "list of some articles made in Birmingham and the hardware districts, which are largely replaced in common markets of the world by the productions of other countries." The author states that "this list might be immensely extended by further investigation, which the shortness of time has not permitted." Among the articles enumerated are hoes—and I ask the attention of the gentleman from New York [Mr. BROOKS]—

"Hoes: for cotton and other purposes, an article of large consumption."

On this article the report remarks:

"The United States compete with us, for their own use and to some extent for export."

Then we have the following:

"Axes: for felling trees, &c., an article of large consumption. The United States supply our colonies and the world with the best article."

Then there are:

"Carpenters' broad-axes; carpenters' and coopers' adzes; coopers' tools, various sorts; shoemakers' hammers and tools."

With regard to these "Germany and the United States" are mentioned as the countries "whose products are believed to have replaced those of England."

Speaking of cut nails, the report says:

"United States export to South America and our colonies."

And, with regard to horseshoe nails, which we protect by a duty of 5 cents per pound, and the manufacture of which under that ample protection has been cheapened and so perfected that this parliamentary report announces that they exclude the English from common markets because they are—

"Beautifully made by machinery in the United States."

Mr. WINANS. Will the gentleman allow me to ask him a question?

Mr. KELLEY. Not at present. I will be glad when I have got a little further into my subject to answer, but not at this point.

Mr. WINANS. My question comes in properly here.

Mr. KELLEY. I will hear the gentleman.

Mr. WINANS. I understand that the purport of what the gentleman has been reading is to show that the United States, notwithstanding the high tariff——

Mr. KELLEY. I do not yield to the gentleman for a speech. If he has a question to put, let him put it squarely.

Mr. WINANS. I merely wished to make a preliminary remark. But, without any preliminaries, my question is this: If, under the operation of our tariff, American manufacturers could compete with British manufacturers in British markets, why should the high tariff be maintained to oppress our own people?

Mr. KELLEY. The gentleman's question will be abundantly answered as I proceed. But I may remark here that if by protection you secure to your capital and industry a certain market, capitalists will invest in the erection of workshops, purchase of machinery, and by high wages will induce skilled and ingenious workmen to leave their homes and accept employment on better terms among strangers. Thus under protection capital has been invested,

and skilled laborers gathered, and our inventive genius has improved the methods of production, until we have come to be able to make the articles mentioned in this list cheaper than free-trade England. But withdraw this protection, and you will enable foreigners, with the immense accumulations of capital they possess, to combine and undersell our home manufacturers for a few years, and thus destroy them. The purpose of a protective tariff is that of the fence around an orchard in a district where cattle are permitted to run at large. I believe I have answered the question of the gentleman.

The gentleman from New York [Mr. BROOKS] said that his heart glowed with pride when in a distant foreign land he saw a camel robed in American muslin. The value of the kind of muslin used for such a purpose is almost all in the cost of the raw material; it is woven of the coarsest yarn. I wish he had been in Abyssinia in 1867; how his pulse would have quickened and his heart expanded as he saw that while England was wreathing the latest glory around her brows by moving an army into the heart of Abyssinia for the relief of a few of her subjects, the ingenuity and protected industry of the United States was providing that army with water from day to day.

For proof of this I turn again to the Parliamentary report. It says: "Pumps of various sorts largely exported from the United States." Note, "an American pump finding water for the Abyssinian expedition." Those pumps, unlike the coarse cotton, the sight of which so rejoiced the gentleman, involved a preponderant percentage of labor—labor for the digging and carrying of the coal, ore, and limestone, and on through successive grades of labor to their completion, so that probably 90 per cent. of their cost was labor. I submit the list entire for the gentleman's consideration.

Appendix No. 22 to the report from the select Committee on Scientific Instruction, together with the proceedings of the committee, minutes of evidence, and appendix.

[Ordered by the House of Commons to be printed 15th July, 1868.]

PAPER HANDED IN BY MR. FIELD.

List of some articles made in Birmingham and the hardware district which are largely replaced in common markets of the world by the productions of other countries:

Articles or class of articles.	Country whose products are believed to have replaced those of this district, in whole or in part.
Carpenters' tools: As hammers, plyers, pincers, compasses, hand and bench vises.	} Germany chiefly.
Chains: Of light description, where the cost is more in labor than in material, as halter chains and bowties, and such like.	} Germany.
Fi -pans of fine finishing	} France.
Wood-handled spades and shovels, an article of very large consumption.	} United States exports them to all our colonies.

LIST—Continued.	
Articles or class of articles.	Country whose products are believed to have replaced those of this district, in whole or in part.
Hoes: For cotton and other purposes, an article of large consumption.	United States compete with us for their own use and to some extent for export.
Axes: For felling trees, &c., an article of large consumption.	United States supply our colonies and the world with the best article.
Carpenters' broadaxes. Carpenters' and coopers' adzes. Coopers' tools, various sorts. Shoemakers' hammers and tools.	Germany and the United States.
Machetes: For cutting sugar canes, an important article.	Believed to be now Germany.
Nails: Cut	United States export to South America and our colonies. Belgium.
Wrought	
Point de Paris (wire nails.)	French and Belgian largely supersede English.
Horse-nails	Beautifully made by machinery in the United States.
Pumps: Of various sorts	Largely exported by United States. [NOTE.—An American pump finding water for the Abyssinian expedition.]
Agricultural implements: Plows, cotton gins, cultivators, kibbling machines, corn-crushers, churns, rice-hullers, mowing machines, hay rakes.	Many articles similar to these are exported by United States to common markets.
Sewing machines	United States.
Lamps: For use with petroleum, now an article of very large consumption.	The United States petroleum lamps supplant the English in India and China.
Lamps for the table	French even imported to England.
Tin-ware: Tinned spoons, cooks' ladles, and various culinary articles of fine manufacture and finish.	France.
Locks: Door locks, chest locks, drawer locks, cupboard locks in great variety. Door latches in great variety.	United States, France, and Germany.
Curry-combs	United States exports to Canada. United States and France.
Traps: Rat, beaver, and fox (twisted.)	United States export to Canada.
Gimlets and augers, (twisted.)	United States export to Canada and probably elsewhere.
Brass-foundery, cast: As hinges, brass hooks, and castors, in great variety; door buttons, sash fasteners, and a great variety of other articles.	These articles, in great variety, are now extensively exported from France and Germany.

LIST—Continued.	
Articles or class of articles.	Country whose products are believed to have replaced those of this district, in whole or in part.
Brass-foundery stamped: As curtain pins and bands, cornices, gilt beading, and a great variety of other brass-foundery.	These articles, in great variety, are now extensively exported from Germany and France.
Needles: An article of large consumption.	Mostly Germany,(Rhenish Prussia,)even imported to England.
Fish-hooks	Believed Germany.
Guns: A great variety of sporting guns, articles of large consumption, formerly entirely from Birmingham.	Now exported largely from Liège, Belgium, and Etienne, France.
Breech-loading muskets and revolver pistols.	United States.
Watches and clocks	Switzerland and France import into England, United States, and France. [NOTE.—Watches made in the United States interchangeable by machinery.]
Iron	Belgium.
Glass: For windows, an article of large consumption; spectacle and all other glass.	Belgium supplants ours in our own colonies.
Table glass.	Believed to be Belgium and France.
Swords	Prussia and Belgium.
Jewelry: Gold, gilt, and fancy steel, in very great variety.	France and Germany. These articles are even imported into England.
Small steel trinkets: As bag and purse clasps, steel buttons, chains, key rings, and other fastenings, and many others in great variety.	France and Germany. Many of those even imported into England.
Leather bags, with clasps, purses, and courier bags, &c.	Austria, France, and Russia. We believe about all these articles sold in England are imported.
Buttons: Mother of pearl	Vienna, imported to England.
Horn	France, imported to England.
Porcelain. (formerly Minton's of Stoke.)	France entirely superseded English, and imported to England largely.
Steel buttons,(formerly Bolton & Watts.)	France.
Florentine or lasting boot-buttons.	Germany.
Steel pens,pen-holders, brass scales and weights.	France.
Iron gas-tubing	Germany.
Elastic belts with metal fastenings.	Germany.
Brass chandeliers and gas-fittings.	France and Prussia.
Harness buckles and furniture. German-silver spoons, forks, &c.	France, Austria, and Prussia.
Locks: Best trunk, door, and cabinet locks.	Prussia and France.

LIST—Continued.

Articles or class of articles.	Country whose products are believed to have replaced those of this district, in whole or in part.
Umbrella furniture	France and Prussia.
Horn combs	Prussia.
Pearl and tortoise shell goods	France and Austria.
Steel wire	Prussia and Belgium.
Iron and brass hooks	Prussia and France.
Japanned articles	Prussia and France.
Hollow wares, enameled	France and Prussia.
Optical instruments. Mathematical instruments.	France, Austria, and Bavaria.
Japanned wares	Germany and France.
Bits and stirrups	Belgium and France.
Coach springs and axle-trees.	France.
Electro-plated wares; (customers preferring French goods.)	France.
Gas-fittings	United States.
Weighing machines	United States.
Plumbers' brass foundery.	United States.
Table glass-ware	United States.
Door locks	United States.
Machines for domestic purposes, as sausage machines, coffee-mills, and washing machines.	United States.
Nuts and bolts	United States.
Penknives and scissors	United States.
Stamped brass ware, (certain kinds)	United States.
American "notions," as baskets, clothes-pegs, washing and agricultural machines.	United States.
Cutlery: In great variety: scissors, light-edge tools, such as chisels, &c.	Germany.
Pins for piano-strings and other small fittings for pianos. Silver wire for binding the bars, strings of pianos, &c.	France.

This list might be immensely extended by further investigation, which the shortness of time has not permitted.

THE INTERNAL REVENUE SYSTEM—IT IS EXPENSIVE AND INQUISITORIAL, AND SHOULD BE ABOLISHED AT THE EARLIEST POSSIBLE DAY.

At a later stage of the debate the gentleman from Ohio [Mr. STEVENSON] presented his views on the general subject. He had previously denounced the protectionists of the House as a faction, and now deplores the fact that "the beautiful idea," free trade, "cannot be wholly realized until the commercial millennium." He will, however, do all he can to hasten its triumph. In this direction he goes further than Calhoun or any southern leader ever went. His is a manufacturing and agricultural district, yet he not only echoes the demand of the gentleman from the free-trade commercial city of New York for free coal, iron, salt, and lumber, and a general reduction of the tariff, but leaps beyond him, and proposes to give permanence to the system of internal taxes, which

was established as a temporary war measure, and which costs annually over $3,000,000, maintains an army of tens of thousands of office-holders, and makes inquisition into the private affairs of every citizen, and would simply remove from it "irritating, petty, useless, and vexatious elements." Sir, the gentleman cannot be ignorant of the fact that every dollar drawn from the people by these taxes is so much added to the cost of the productions of the farm and workshop, and operates as a bonus to the foreign competitors of our farmers and mechanics in common markets. But even this will not content him. He grieves that other and more onerous taxes cannot constitutionally be levied on the farms, workshops, and homes of the people of Ohio and the rest of the country. On this point he gives forth no uncertain sound. He hopes the Constitution will yet be so amended as to constrain every owner of a farm or cross-road's blacksmith shop to make the acquaintance of a collector of United States taxes. On this point he said:

"In fact, I incline to the opinion that one of the errors committed by our forefathers in framing the Constitution—and since we have amended it in such material matters lately, we can afford to say that they did commit some errors in framing it—was in not permitting direct taxation upon property according to its value. And some day I trust the Constitution will permit the Government to levy taxes upon property according to its value. But until that day, as long as the debt remains a material burden, we must, in my judgment, retain the less objectionable and burdensome parts of both systems of taxation."

Mr. STEVENSON. I want to know whether the gentleman does not consider that the material part of the internal revenue taxes must be continued while the debt remains?

Mr. KELLEY. No, sir. I believe that if gentlemen will adopt the tariff bill now under consideration, extended as is its free list and great as are the reductions in rates of duties, we can take the internal taxes off all but eight articles by a law of this session and go still further in that direction during the next session.

Mr. STEVENSON. What articles are they?

Mr. KELLEY. I will come to that in the course of my remarks. I have a note of them. While on this subject let me say that I believe further, that in the interest of the farmers of the country we should hasten the day when we can take the tax off distilled spirits.

Sir, the West has grain for which she can find no market. The Governments of Great Britain and France, coöperating with our internal tax system, deprive them of what would be a generous market. Take the tax of 65 cents a gallon off whisky, and the grain now rotting in the granaries of the West would be distilled into alcohol and shipped to the countries of South America, the West India Islands, Turkey, and elsewhere. I have now answered the gentleman as far as I propose to at present. I have, however, not yet done with him.

Mr. STEVENSON. The gentleman is criticising _wh_ a_t_ was drawn out of me by a question from himself. I ask him in fairness to permit me to put a question to him.

Mr. KELLEY. Well, go on.

Mr. STEVENSON. I want to know whether the gentleman is not in favor, before reducing the tariff on coal and iron, of taking the internal revenue tax off whisky and abolishing the tax on incomes entirely?

Mr. KELLEY. I am in favor of abolishing at the earliest possible day a system that makes inquisition into the private affairs of every man and women in the country, and has cost us for the three last years an average of $8,509,532 77 per annum, and taken probably 10,000 persons from industrial employments and fastened them as vampires upon the people. That is what I am in favor of. But I hold the floor for another purpose than a mere controversy with the gentleman.

Mr. STEVENSON. Then the gentleman declines to answer my question.

Mr. KELLEY. I have answered the gentleman's question, and every gentleman present will, I think, say I have answered it frankly.

FREE TRADE MEANS LOW WAGES AND A LIMITED MARKET FOR GRAIN.

Mr. Chairman, I am not specially familiar with the gentleman's district. Though I have visited Cincinnati several times and ridden through Hamilton county, I have but few acquaintances within their limits; yet I know something about them. The last annual report of the Cincinnati Board of Trade informs us that during the year ending March 31, 1869, there were produced in the gentleman's district and the adjoining one, in about 3,000 separate establishments, 187 distinct classes of manufactured articles, of an aggregate value of $104,657,612. The cash capital invested in these establishments, the report says, is $49,824,124, and they give employment to 55,275 hands.

Mr. Chairman, I venture the remark that there is not among these 55,275 working people one who will indorse the opinions advanced by the gentleman.

Mr. STEVENSON. Will the gentleman yield to me for a moment?

Mr. KELLEY. No, sir; I must decline.

Mr. STEVENSON. The gentleman holds the floor without restriction by the courtesy of the House.

Mr. KELLEY. I will yield further to the gentleman during the course of my remarks, but not at present.

Many of the laboring people of his district are immigrants and know how small are the wages of workmen on the other side of the Atlantic, and how humble the fare on which they live. They know that free trade means low wages. Buy labor where you can buy it cheapest is the cardinal maxim of the free trader. More than 85 per cent. of the cost of every ton of coal, salt, and pig iron is in the wages of labor, and when the gentleman shall have stricken the duties off these articles, the 1,500,000 people who are now earning good wages in their production must compete with the cheap labor of Turk's Island, England, Wales, and Germany. Thrown out of remunerative employment in the trades to which they have devoted their lives, as they will be, they must compete with workmen in other pursuits, even though they glut the market and bring down the general rate of wages throughout the land. He who advocates protective duties pleads the cause of the American laborer. I will not amplify this proposition. I regard it as a truism, and beg leave to illustrate it by inviting the attention of my colleague [Mr. ALLISON] from Iowa, and the gentleman from Ohio, to a statement of the wages and subsistence of families of laborers in Europe, on page 179 of the monthly report of the Deputy Special Commissioner of the Revenue, No. 4 of the series 1869-70. It refers specially to Germany, and was translated and compiled from Nos. 10-12 of the publications of the royal Prussian statistical bureau, Berlin, 1868.

This paper, gentlemen will remark, was not prepared for or by American politicians, or by a faithless officer of this Government, or by any representative of a free-trade or protective league. Its facts are most significant.

The wheat-growers of Iowa and the West are suffering from the want of a market for their grain. Too large a proportion of our people are raising wheat. We want more miners, railroad men, and mechanics, and our present rates of wages are inducing them to come to us. Half a million people tempted by these wages will come this year. Our working people are free consumers of wheat, beef, pork, and mutton. But could they be, under free trade or reduced duties? These articles are luxuries rarely enjoyed by the working people of England or the continent, with whom anti-protectionists would compel them to compete. The official paper to which I refer tells us that "rye and potatoes form the chief food of the laboring classes; that the wives and daughters of brick-makers, coal and iron miners, and furnace and rolling-mill men aid them in their rough employments; that the regular wages of workingmen average in summer and winter from 16$\frac{4}{5}$ to 24 cents per day, and those of females from 8$\frac{1}{4}$ to 14$\frac{1}{2}$ cents per day; that miners at tunneling are sometimes paid as much as 72 cents (1 thaler) per day, and that a brick-maker, aided by his wife, averages 80 cents per day; that wages for female labor are more uniform, and that 18 cents per day can be earned by a skillful hand; that juvenile laborers in factories begin with 48 cents per week for ten hours daily, and rise to 72 cents per week; that the general average of daily wages is as follows: males, for twelve hours' work per day in the country, 19$\frac{1}{4}$ cents; in cities, 24 cents; and that the wages of master-workmen, overseers, &c., are at least $172 per year." That gentlemen and their constituents may study this instructive paper I beg leave to submit it entire to the reporters.

Wages and subsistence of families of laborers in Europe.

GERMANY.

Lower Silesia, translated and compiled from No. 10-12 of the publications of the Royal Prussian Statistical Bureau, Berlin, 1868.

The regular wages of workingmen average in summer and winter from 16.8 cents to 24 cents (gold) per day; of females, from 08.4 to 14.4 cents per day, more nearly approaching the higher rate. During the short winter days workingmen receive for 8 hours' labor from 10 to 14.4 cents; the females, 7.2 cents; while in summer, for 12 to 13 hours' labor the relative wages are from 19.2 to 28.8 cents, and from 14.4 to 19.2 cents, respectively. The wages of those working in the royal forests are so regulated as to average 24 cents per day for males, and 14.4 cents per day for females; in some mountain countries the latter receive but 12 cents.

In larger cities wages rise above these rates, especially for skilled labor. Men working on railroads receive in summer from 28.8 to 36 cents per day; and women from 16.8 to 26.4 cents. In the larger cities ordinary female help in housekeeping is paid from 24 to 26.4 cents.

Work done by the piece or by contract is paid about one third more than the customary wages. A common laborer expects in contract work from 36 to 48 cents; at railroad work even more.

When work is scarce the wages often fall to about 16.8 cents per day for males, and 9.6 cents for females.

Labor is often paid by the hour, at from 01.4 to 3 cents for males, and 0.4 to 2 cents for females; 2.4 cents per hour are the wages of an able field laborer in the mountains.

During the summer especially, opportunities for work are offered to children, who receive from 6.11 to 7.2 cents per day, and in winter about 4.8 cents.

Wherever the work rises above mere manual labor in a trade or factory, the daily wages of men are from 30 to 48 cents, and often rise to 60 cents. Miners at tunneling are frequently paid 72 cents, (1 thaler;) in the district of Görlitz, a brick-maker aided by his wife, averages 80 cents per day; in the district of Fauer from $5 76 to $7 20 per week. Skilled workmen of large experience receive from $360 to $432 per annum. The wages of the molders and enamelers in iron founderies, of the locksmiths and joiners in machine-works, in piano factories, amount to from 72 cents to $1 08 per day; the same in manufactories of glass, silverware, watches, and hat factories. The highest wages paid to a very skillful joiner in a pianoforte factory were $12 24 per week.

Wages for female labor are more uniform throughout; 18 cents per day can be earned by a skillful hand, 24 cents per day very rarely.

Juvenile laborers in factories begin with wages of 48 cents per week, for 10 hours' work daily, and rise to 72 cents per week. The law prohibits the employment of children under 12 years of age; from 12 to 14 years it permits 6 hours, and from 14 to 16 years, 10 hours' daily labor.

The general average of daily wages is as follows: Males, for 12 hours' work per day, in the country, 19.2 cents: in cities, 24 cents; harder labor, 30 cents; in cities, 36 cents; skilled labor, 60 cents.

The wages of master workmen, overseers, &c., are not included in the above average, but are at least $172 per annum.

In regard to the time of work, laborers in factories are employed 11 to 12 hours per day, (exclusive of time for meals;) where work is continued day and night, the hours for the day are from 6 to 12 a. m., and 1 to 7 p. m.; for the night, from 7 p. m. to 6 a. m., with ¼ hour recess; in a few districts 10 hours constitute a day's work. In many cloth factories and wool spinneries, males and females work 12 to 13 hours, and some even 16 hours per day. As an example, a cloth factory employs firemen and machinists 16 hours, spinners and dyers 14 hours, all others 12 hours, exclusive of time for meals. In glass-works, the nature of the work requires from 16 to 18 hours for melters, 13 to 15 hours for blowers; but then one party rests while the other works. Rye and potatoes form the chief food of the laboring classes.

Savings.

Although but few workingmen can save any portion of their earnings, still there are some who purchase a little piece of land, a house, or a cow, and the latest accounts from fifteen districts in Lower Silesia show deposits in savings-banks from house servants of $428,455; of apprentices and mechanical workmen of $124,522. No statistics of savings of factory workers were obtained. In some factories the workmen have established savings-banks, some of which have deposits of from $3,000 to $10,000.

DETAILED STATEMENTS OF THE WAGES AND COST OF LIVING IN DIFFERENT DISTRICTS OF LOWER SILESIA.

1. *District of Bolkenhain.*

The annual expenses of a family of about 5 persons, (3 children,) belonging to the working class, were as follows:

Provisions, (per day, 0.144 to 0.163,) per year.....	$60 00
Rent, (8 thalers,).................................	5 76
Fuel	3 60
Clothing, linen, &c...............................	14 40
Furniture, tools, &c..............................	7 20
Taxes: State 0.72; church 12; commune 36, $1 20	
School for 2 children.................. 2 50	
	3 70
Total..............................	$94 66

The expenses of a laborer's family being 24 to 26.4 cents per day, the earnings should be 28 to 30.8 cents per day, which the head of the family cannot earn. While his earnings are from 17 to 19 cents, the wife earns 8 to 10 cents, and the children must help as soon as old enough. Miners in this district have 24 to 29 cents daily wages; factory men from 19 to 29 cents; mechanics receive 48 to 54 cents per week, besides board; male house servants $17 to $30, and female $12 per annum, exclusive of board and lodging.

2. *District of Landeshut.*

Expenses of a family:

	In the country..	In a city.
Rent per annum........................	$5 76	$10 72
Provisions (per week, 90 cents,) per annum................	46 80*	56 10
Fuel and light per annum.........	14 40	16 42
Taxes, &c., per annum.............	3 60	4 32
Clothing, &c., per annum..........	8 56	10 00
Other expenses per annum.......	7 20	8 57
Total..................................	$86 32	$106 13

The income of laborers' (weavers') families does generally not reach these amounts. Many are permitted to gather their wood from the royal forests, and spend little for clothing, which they beg from charitable neighbors. A weaver earns here from 48 to 72 cents, $1 and $1 50 per week; most weavers have 2 looms in operation, and together with their wives earn from $1 50 to $2 16 per week. The average earnings of weavers are given at 96 cents per week, or about $50 per annum.

3. *District of Hirschberg.*

The lowest cost of living for a laborer's family is given at $64 80 to $72 per annum, of which are expended for provisions $43 30, for clothing $17, taxes $3 16, fuel $3 60, rent $4, &c. In the summer the wages for 12 hours' daily work, for males, are from 15 to 39 cents; for females 5 to 17 cents per day; in winter from 3 to 7 cents less. A male farm hand receives $12 to $22 per year; a boy $9 to $14; a maid-servant $12 to $18 per annum, with board.

The annual expenses of a laborer's family, living in a comfortable manner, without luxuries, would be nearly double the amount actually expended above.

*Per week, $1 08.

The following is an estimate:

Rent, (one room, alcove, and bed-room,)	$8 64
Fuel and light	14 40
Provisions, (breakfast, coffee; at noon, potatoes, dumpling—10 cents; evening, bread, a little brandy—5 cents; supper, soup, bread, vegetables—6 cents,)	75 00
Clothing, (husband $6 48, wife $5 76, children $7 20; soap 72 cents,)	20 16
Taxes, &c	2 16
Schooling of children, (2½ cents per week per child,)	3 60
School books	72
To lay by for sickness, &c	8 58
Unforeseen expenses	8 58
Total	$141 84

4. District of Schönau.

The ordinary yearly wages, in addition to board, paid to servants in this rural district, were as follows: Man-servant, $14 40 to $21 60; boys, $8 64 to $12 96; maid-servants, $8 64 to $17 28; children's nurses, $5 76 to $12 96.

During the harvest the daily wages for 14 hours' work are as follows: Mowers, from 19.2 to 28.8 cents; laborers, (males,) from 19.2 to 24 cents; females, from 14.4 to 17 cents.

In other seasons males receive for 10 hours' daily labor from 14.4 to 19.2 cents, and females 12 to 14.4 cents per day; and in winter males receive 12 cents, and females 7.4 to 9.6 cents. A laborer in the cities receives 24 to 28.8 cents per day; the "fellows" (journeymen) of trades receive from 60 cents to $1 20 per week, and board.

A laborer's family of 5 persons requires for its subsistence during the year the following amount: For provisions, $72 to $85 72; rent of 1 room and 3 bedrooms, $4 32; clothing, &c., $10 80; fuel, &c., $3 60; taxes, &c., $3 60. Total, $103 04.

5. District of Goldberg.

The cost of living of a laborer's family, (husband, wife, and two children,) in this district is thus given: Provisions, $75 60; rent, $4 32; fuel, $7 20; clothing, $10 02; furniture, tools, &c., 72 cents; taxes, &c., $2 28. Total, $100 14. In less expensive times provisions have been estimated at $20 less.

In the rural portion men receive 21.6 cents, women 14.4 cents for a day's work; this average includes higher wages for skilled labor.

On a farm a man-servant receives $17 20 per year, in addition to board, &c., which may be estimated at $43 20; a maid-servant receives $14 40, besides board.

Laborers in stone-quarries earn from 24 to 43.2 cents per day; in cloth factories 1.8 to 2.2 cents per hour, while the daily wages of carpenters are from 33.6 to 38.4 cents: masons, 33.6 to 45.6 cents; roof-slaters, 33.6 to 45.6.

Shoemakers and tailors receive from 9 to 10 cents, besides their board and lodging, which is valued at 12 cents.

6. District of Löwenberg.

The yearly expenses of a family with 3 children are estimated at from $93 60 to $103, namely:

	In city.	In country.
Rent	$10 60	$4 32
Provisions, ($1 20 per week,)	62 40	55 72
Fuel and light	12 66	10 80
Taxes, school, &c	3 60	3 60
Clothing, &c	12 85	12 85
Other expenses	5 76	5 76
Total	$107 87	$93 05

Wages are as follows:

Men, day laborers, from 14.4 to 28.8 cents per day; women 12 to 18 cents per day; men, with board, 9.6 to 14.4 cents per day; women, with board, 7.2 to 12 cents per day. From 10 to 14 hours constitute a day's labor; more hours, and harder work secure higher wages.

Male servants per year, $14 40 to $36, and board; female, per year, $8 57 to $21 60, and board.

Journeymen in trades obtain the following:

Wages per week, (with board and lodging.)	In cities.		In the country.	
	Minimum.	Maximum.	Minimum.	Maximum.
	Cents.	Cents.	Cents.	Cents.
Smiths	54	72	42	72
Wheelwrights	54	72	42	72
Shoemakers	54	60	42	72
Tailors	54	72	30	66
Cabinet-makers	54	72	42	72

7. City of Greifenberg.

The subsistence of a workingman's family, consisting of 5—man, wife, and 3 children—is thus given:

Income.

A mason receives 33.6 cents per day, regular work, 32 weeks in a year	$64 52
Weaving or other work, 4 months, at 48 to 60 cents per week, say	8 00
Yearly earnings of wife	7 20
Total	$79 72

A day laborer receives 24 cents per day, or $1 44 per week, regular work 40 weeks	$57 60
During the rest of the year he and his wife may earn	14 40
Total	$72 00

A carpenter earns a little more than a mason, his chances for winter labor being better. A weaver, working at home, makes less than the day laborer; those in the factory earn per year $72.

Expenses of a family.

Rent, $8 64; clothing, $14 40, (shoes being a large item;) light, $1 44; fuel, $5 04; repairing tools, 72 cents; taxes, $1 44; school for three children, $1 44. Total, $33 12.

Provisions.—The meals consist of potatoes and bread, their means not being sufficient to allow meat; potatoes, 20 bushels, $10 08; bread, (6 cents per day,) $21 90; coffee, (chicory, 4 pounds per day,) $2 88; butter, (¼ pound per week,) lard, herring, salt, (24 cents per week,) $12 48. Total, $47 26. Aggregate expenses, $80 38.

Note.—If the work is not regular, the demands of the family must be curtailed, and suffering often takes place.

8. District of Görlitz.

Here the condition of the laborer appears more comfortable, since work can be found throughout the year.

Masons and carpenters earn 36 to 43.4 cents per day; railroad laborers, 26.4 to 28.8; field laborers, 21.6 to 28.8, and females, 14.5 to 24.

The lowest expenses for a family consisting of 4 or 5 persons are thus computed:

Provisions	$57 60	to	$65 72
Rent, lights, and fuel	11 52	to	21 10
Clothing	13 57	to	18 00
Tools, &c	1 44	to	2 88
School	1 44	to	2 88
Taxes	72	to	1 44
Total	$86 29	to	$132 52

By careful inquiries it has been reliably ascertained that a family can earn from $93 60 to $144 a year, so that some lay up small savings.

For the city of Görlitz the average income of a laborer's family is estimated at $95 to $144 a year;

the expenses for 4 or 5 persons, from $115 to $172 80, namely:

Rent, light, and fuel	$22 72 to	$32 15
Clothing, &c	14 40 to	21 60
Tools, furniture, &c	1 44 to	5 76
School	4 32 to	5 04
Provisions	72 00 to	108 25
Total	$114 88 to	$172 80

9. *District of Glogau.*

Farm laborers' income:

Males— 6 weeks in harvest, at 30 cents per
day.. $10 80
14 weeks, (sowing and haymaking,) at
24 cents per day........................... 20 16
15 weeks, fall and spring, at 18 cents
per day.. 16 20
15 weeks, winter, at 14.4 per day........ 12 96

Total, 50 weeks.............................. 60 12

Females— 6 weeks, at 12 cents per day (5 days
per week) $3 60
14 weeks, at 9.6 cents per day... 6 72
15 weeks, at 8.4 per day......... 6 30
15 weeks, at 7.2 per day......... 5 40
22 02

Total, 50 weeks................................ $82 14

Expenses of a family with 3 children:

16 sheffels* rye, at $1 32	$21 12
2 sheffels wheat, at $1 80	3 60
2 sheffels barley, at $1 20	2 40
2 sheffels peas, at $1 44	2 88
2 sheffels millet, at $1 44	2 88
24 bags potatoes, at 38.4 cents	9 22
52 pounds butter, at 19.2 cents	9 98
18 quarts salt, at .24 cents	4 40
Meat, (.2 quarters mutton, $3 60, 1 pig, $10 80)	14 40
52 pounds salt, at .024	1 25
Rent, $5 76, light, $1 52	7 28
Fuel, (wood, $9 72, coal, $3 18)	12 90
Clothing	18 72
Taxes, and other expenses	8 00
Total	$119 03

As, according to these statistics a man and wife can earn but $82 14 per year, a deficiency of $36 89 must be made up by the work of the children or by extra labor in the summer, especially at harvest time.

15. *District of Leignitz.*

Expenses of a family with 3 children:

Provisions—
Bread, 1 pound flour per head daily........... $26 52
Potatoes, ⅓ bag or 75 pounds per week at 18
cents.. 9 36

Carried over $35 88

* 1 sheffel equals 1.56 bushel, United States.

Brought over	$35 88
Barley, 2 sheffels, at 90 cents	0 96
Peas, 1 sheffel, at $1 08	1 08
Butter, 1 to 1¾ pound per week, 71¼ pounds per year, at 19 cents	13 73
Milk, 4 quarts daily, at 4 cents	5 84
Meat, 1 swine for fattening, or 1 pound per week	5 56
Salt, 1 pound per week, at 2.4 cents	1 25
Coffee, chiccory, sugar	4 32
Wheat flour for cake on holidays	1 32
Beer	90
Rent, for a room, a garret-room and small space, per annum	7 20
Light, oil for 26 to 30 weeks, ¼ to ¾ pound at 6 cents	2 34
Fuel, during 6 winter months, 20 cents summer, 10 cents per week	8 00

Clothing—
Husband: 2 shirts, at 72 cents...........$1 44
1 pair boots...................... 2 88
pantaloons, (3 pairs in 2 years) 72
coat, &c........................ 72
5 76

Wife: 2 chemises.....................$1 44
1 pair shoes.................. 1 20
Dress, &c................... 2 64
5 28

Children: 2 shirts, at 36 cents each.. 2 16
3 pairs shoes................ 2 16
clothing..................... 2 16
6 48

Soap for washing............................. 1 20
18 72

Tools, for repair of............................. 1 43
Taxes—income, 72 cents; communal, .384 cents;
school, including books, $2.556................ 3 60

Total expenses $112 13

Income of a family with two children:

Husband averages 305 days, at 21.6 cents	$65 88
Wife averages 250 days, at 10.4 cents	26 00
Oldest child averages 60 days, at 7.2 cents	4 32

Every married workman receives:

1 sheffel wheat	$1 80
2 sheffels rye	2 16
2 sheffels barley	1 92
1 sheffel peas	1 08
	6 96

He can raise on a patch of land 10 bags potatoes, valued at	2 88
And glean at harvest 3 sheffels of rye or barley	3 06
For extra work through the year	8 64
For a fat pig	5 76

Total income $123 50

In the city of Liegnitz the average expense of a laborer's family is estimated at $141 84 per year.

Table showing the rates of wages paid for factory and other labor in Lower Silesia during the year 1868.

[Rates expressed in cents, (gold,) United States.]

Branches and occupations.	Wages per day.			Branches and occupations.	Wages per day.		
	Males.	Females.	Children.		Males.	Females.	Children.
Bleaching presses:				Earthenware, &c.:			
Ordinary hands	18 to 36	14½ to 18		potter-turners	48		
Bleachers	27 to 33			foremen	96		
Manglers	36 to 42			Glass-works, polishers			
Foremen	48 to 60			molders	60	10 to 24	
Browers	24 to 36			painters and gilders	40 to 72	18 to 36	
Brickyards:				skilled hands	60 to 96		
Ordinary work	20 to 24			bottle-makers	48 to 60		
Molders	29 to 39			ordinary hands	24 to 36	12 to 18	12
Chamotte-molders	33 to 48			Flour mills:			
Contract work	36 to 60			Laborers	22 to 29		
Average summer wages	24 to 42			Assistant millers	36 to 60		
Cane factories:				Firemen	24 to 29		
Turners	36 to 66			Machinists	33		
Engravers	36 to 60			Foremen	72		
Joiners	48			Gas-works, laborers	24 to 36	24 to 36	
Laborers	28 to 42			Hatters:			
Chemical works:				Ordinary hands	48 to $1		
Average wages	31½	8 to 15	4 to 6	Skilled hands	$1 66 to $2		
Fireworks	24 to 33			Iron-works:			
Cigar factories:				Laborers	18 to 23		
Foremen	44			Locksmiths	24 to 60		
Strippers	-	16 to 18	6 to 10	Machine-builders	60 to $1 08		
Skilled hands	$1 to $2	24 to 40		Molders	42 to 72		
Box-makers	12			Turners	52 to 72		
Wrappers	-	18 to 24		Machinists	40 to 72		
Rollers	24 to 72			Foremen	72		
Assorters	72 to $1 08			Watchmen	48		
Packers	36 to 48			Enamelers	36 to 72		
Foremen	$1 50			Cutters	60 to 72		
Distillers	18 to 36			Lime kilns:			
Dyeing establishments:				Laborers, in winter	20 to 30		
Garden	20 to 54	14 to 18		in summer	24 to 36		
Fullers	24	15		Mining:			
Shearers	29 to 36			Ordinary labor	18 to 24	12	16 to 20
Foremen	$1 08			Miners	48 to 60		
Earthenware, &c.:				Drivers	38	10	
Pottery, molders	60 to 72	14 to 22		Oil refiners	18 to 42		
ordinary work	24 to 60			Paper mills:			
Stoneware, ordinary work	18 to 21			Ordinary laborers	21 to 48	10 to 24	8 to 16
turners	24 to 48			Cutters	24		
painters	24 to 42			Holland-miller	30		
Porcelain, glazing makers	30 to 35	18 to 24		Foremen	36 to 60		
burners	30 to 42			Machinists	36		
gilders	36 to 42	12 to 18		Bookbinders	32 to 58		

	42 to 48	12 to 24		60 to 84 / 24 to 72	28 to 30	12 to 15 / 15
Printers				60 to 84 / 24 to 72		
Railroad-car shop:						
Smiths	40 to 72					
Locksmiths	36 to 96					
Railroad-car shop:						
Tanners	42 to $1 08					
Screw-cutters	30 to 60					
Tinners	42 to 60					
File-cutters	48 to 72					
Wheelwrights	48 to 96					
Carpenters	42 to 66					
Painters	48 to 66					
Upholsterers	36 to 60					
Laborers	34					
Foremen	36					
Starch factories.............	18 to 36		12 to 17			
	36					

		60 to 84 / 24 to 72	28 to 30	12 to 15 / 15
Silveremith.				
Watch-factory workmen.				
Saw-mills				
Laborers	26 to 48			0 55
Locksmiths	36 to 60			0 55
Machinists	48			
Foremen				
Spinning flax	24 to 42	12 to 30	12 to 24	
cotton	20 to 42	12 to 18	14 to 24	9 to 12
wool	18 to 48	14 to 24	9 to 15	6 to 18
Sugar refiners	14 to 36	9 to 15	12 to 15	
Tanners	36 to 60	12 to 15		
Toy factories:				
Ordinary laborers...........	18 to 36			
Turners	36 to 48	10 to 24		
Sculptors	36 to $1 08			

The wages of journeymen in the following trades, including board and lodging, are as follows:

Per week.

Bakers........................	$0 92
Butchers......................	0 72
Smiths........................	1 08
Tinners.......................	2 52
Wheelwrights..................	2 16
Furriers......................	2 16
Saddlers......................	0 72
Locksmiths....................	2 52
Tailors.......................	2 52
Shoemakers....................	1 44
Fresco-painters...............	3 42
Cabinet-makers................	2 88 to 3 60
Cloth-weavers.................	1 44 to 2 16

From the reports of the chambers of commerce of Germany the following labor statistics are collected:

In the coal mines of Rhenish-Prussia, average daily wages of 3,661 laborers, with families of 8,572 persons, males $0 64

Iron foundry, (Duisburg,) average wages per day, founders ..... 0 65 to 0 72

Other skilled workmen 0 54

Laborers 0 43

Machinists and locksmiths 0 58

In two iron foundries, same district, average daily wages, respectively ..... 0 53 and 0 65

Iron-bridge establishment 0 55

Safe factory, average yearly earnings 182 80

Zinc establishments, average wages, first-class hands 0 94

Second-class hands 0 72

Other laborers 0 53

Cotton factories, average wages per hand, including children 0 41

Cotton spinning, average wages per hand, (mostly young persons) 0 36

Average weekly wages paid in the coal mines of Plauen, Saxony: to miners, $3 10; to laborers, $1 98, and to boys 40 cents.

[From report of Chamber of Commerce of Chemnitz for 1868.]

SAXONY.

Table showing the average weekly wages of labor paid in the district of Chemnitz, Saxony, in the respective years 1860 and 1864 to 1868. Rates expressed in United States gold values.

Trades.	Males.						Females or (‡) children.					
	1860.	1864.	1865.	1866.	1867.	1868.	1860.	1864.	1865.	1866.	1867.	1868.
Accordeon-makers	$2 16	$6 60	$2 52	$2 52	$2 52	$2 52	$1 08	$1 08	$0 96	$0 90	$0 96	$0 90
Artificial-flower makers	1 08	1 44	2 40	2 16	2 52	2 40		1 08	87	87	87	87
Bakers	1 17	72	2 16	2 16	2 52	2 88						
Barbers	1 80	2 52	48	48	1 44	1 44						
Basket-makers			1 92	1 92								
Barrel-makers	3 24	3 60	3 60	3 60	3 60	3 60						
Beer-brewers	1 08	1 44	2 16	2 88	2 88	3 24	1 44	1 44	1 44	1 44	1 44	1 44
Belt-makers, workers in bronze	2 28	2 52	2 88	2 88	2 88	4 32						
Bleachers	2 04	3 24	2 40	2 40	2 88	2 88	1 20	1 44				
Bookbinders	2 52	2 16	3 12	2 40	2 64	4	1 08	1 44				
Brass-founders	1 80	3 24	72	72	72	56						
Brushmakers	2 52	2 52	2 88	2 88	2 88	2 88						
Bricklayers	2 52	2 52	3 24	3 24	3 60	3 60	1 08	1 08	1 08	1 08	1 08	1 08
Brickmakers	1 08	2 52	2 16	2 33	2 88	2 88						
Butchers	2 88	2 52	2 88	2 88	2 88	2 88	1 08	1 20				
Button-makers	2 16	2 24	2 52	2 52	2 88	2 88	68	1 20				
Card (playing) makers	2 16	2 88	2 16	2 16	2 16	2 16						
Card (carding) makers	2 64	2 76	2 70	2 79	3 24	3 24	1 20	1 44	1 08	1 08	1 20	1 20
Cabinet-makers	3 24	3 24	2 52	2 52	2 16	2 40	90	1 08	72	72	48	2 16
Carpenters	2 78	2 78	2 16	2 16	2 40	2 88	72	96				
Cartoon-makers	2 16	2 16	2 52	2 52	2 88	2 88						
Cigar-makers	1 62	1 98	2 40	72	2 40	2 40	90	1 08	‡96	‡96	‡96	‡96
Chair-framers	2 37	2 37	3 24	3 24	3 24	3 24	72	72	84	84	84	84
Chemical manufacturers	2 04	2 40	2 88	2 88	3 12	3 60		1 62	‡48			‡58
Cloth-finishers	1 80	2 52	2 24	2 88	2 88	2 88	1 44	1 08				
Cloth-weavers	3 24	2 16	2 16	2 16	2 16	3 60		72				
Cloth-shearers	1 08	1 20	1 44	1 44	1 44	1 44						
Cloth-printers	2 16	2 88	1 44	3 60	80	80						
Comb-makers	2 40	2 88	3 88	3 88	3 60	3 60	1 08	1 20	1 08		1 08	1 80
Confectioners	4 32	5 04	4 32	5 04	5 04	5 04						
Coopers	1 68	1 92	2 07	2 16	2 16	2 34						
Cotton-spinners	3 18	3 18	1 44	1 44	1 44	1 44						
Crockery-ware artists	1 44	3 60	3 60	3 60	3 60	3 60						
Crockery-ware workmen	3 16	3 88	3 88	3 88	3 88	3 88						
Day laborers	1 98	2 16	2 16	2 16	2 16	2 16						

Furriers

Gardeners

Glaziers

Glass-workers

Glove-sewers

Goldsmiths

Gunsmiths

Hatters

Harness-makers

Iron and steel workers:

Iron-founders

Machine-builders

Locksmiths

Iron and steel workers:

Cutlers

Nailmakers

Blacksmiths

Screw-makers

Lithographers

Loom-builders

Milliners

Mining:

Carpenters

Miners

Drawers

Day laborers

Needlemakers

Oil-cloth makers

Potters

Printers:

Compositors

Boys

Rope-makers

Saddlers

Saw-mill laborers

Slaters

Shoemakers

Shoemakers' tools

Soap-makers

Stocking-weavers, (machine)

Stonemasons

Stonecutters

Stone quarrymen

Tailors

Turners

Tapestry-makers

Watchmakers

Wheelwright

Worsted work

Wire-cloth makers

Weavers, (silk)

Wool combers

My colleague [Mr. TOWNSEND] hands me a letter containing a statement of American wages in some of the same branches of labor. That gentlemen may contrast them with the wages of Germany, as set forth by the statistical bureau of Prussia, I will hand the letter to the reporters:

PHŒNIXVILLE, PENNSYLVANIA,
March 21, 1870.

DEAR SIR: Your favor of the 16th is before me. Below I give you the prices paid per day to our principal workmen, as follows:

Rolling-mill on rails and beams.

	Per day.		Per day.
Heaters....................	$4 50	*Bar mill.*	
Helpers....................	1 70	Heaters....................	$3 87
Extra helpers..........	1 60	Helpers....................	1 70
Finishing rollerman,	6 75	Rollers....................	2 12
Roughing rollerman,	2 70	Catchers..................	1 55
Catchers..................	2 25	Hooks....................	1 60
Hooks.....................	1 80		
Hot straighteners....	2 50	*Heavy merchant iron.*	
Cold straighteners...	3 60	Heaters....................	4 37
Stochers..................	2 35	Helpers....................	1 70
Pilors......................	1 50	Finishing roller.......	5 00
Laborers..................	1 50	Roughers.................	2 35
Engineers................	2 10	Catcher...................	1 50
		Straightener...........	1 50
Merchant iron.		Mauler....................	1 50
Heaters....................	4 37	Engineer.................	1 90
Helper.....................	1 70		
Extra helpers..........	1 60	*Puddling.*	
Finishing roller.......	4 05	Puddler..................	3 00
Roughing roller......	2 12	Puddler's helpers....	2 00
Catchers..................	1 60		
Roughing catcher....	1 30	*Labor.*	
Straightener...........	1 90	Common labor.........	1 40
Engineers................	2 80		

I am unable to give the wages paid for the above classes of work either in England, France, or Belgium, but I am satisfied from the prices, as we have had them from time to time from these, that their present pay is not over an average of 40 per cent. of above.

Respectfully,
JOHN GRIFFIN,
General Superintendent.

Hon. WASHINGTON TOWNSEND.

Mr. ALLISON. Will the gentleman yield to me for a question?

Mr. KELLEY. Yes, sir.

Mr. ALLISON. I will ask the gentleman whether that is not a report of wages paid by a company that manufactures what are known as iron beams for vessels and bridges?

Mr. KELLEY. They manufacture beams, rails, and other heavy forms of iron.

Mr. ALLISON. And is it not a company which with three others has agreed upon an established list of prices for that class of articles, which prices embarce the prices abroad, together with the tariff duty and a profit on the cost of manufacture?

Mr. KELLEY. I cannot answer the question, because I do not know. I can, however, say that I have never heard such an allegation. But, my dear sir, I do not care what they have agreed to do, if they are thereby enabling American workingmen to keep their children at school, well fed and comfortably clad, to maintain their seats in church, and to lay by something for old age and a rainy day, and not compelling them, as German workmen in like employments are compelled to do, to take their wives and daughters as colaborers into iron and coal mines and furnaces and rolling-mills, so that they may together earn enough to eke out a miserable subsistence.

Mr. ALLISON. I do not take issue with the gentleman upon that question, but merely desire to call his attention to the fact that this is one of four establishments that have a monopoly in this business.

Mr. KELLEY. A monopoly! A workman a monopolist! A poor workman for wages a monopolist! A man who is earning daily wages by hard work in a mine, a furnace, or a rolling-mill will hardly be regarded as a monopolist, though his pay may be ten times what he could get in his native town. No, sir; such men are not monopolists, though free traders constantly denounce them as such.

CINCINNATI—HER WORKSHOPS AND WORKMEN.

Mr. Chairman, 90 per cent. of the cost of iron in all its forms is the wages of labor, and the wages of labor go very largely into wheat and pork and mutton and beef that are eaten, and woolen clothes that are worn by the workmen and their families. The wages of well-paid laborers thus find their way to the pockets of the farmer and the wool-grower.

Mr. STEVENSON. Will the gentleman yield to me now for a question?

Mr. KELLEY. Yes, sir.

Mr. STEVENSON. It seems that the gentleman has just discovered that there are some manufacturers in Cincinnati. I want to know whether he has not also discovered that more than half of the capital and labor and production of those manufactories are in the articles of wood, iron, leather, and paper, upon which I want the duties reduced, and whether it is not to the interest of those producers to have cheap raw material?

Mr. KELLEY. It is the interest of the working people of Cincinnati that the general rate of wages shall be maintained at the highest point. It is not for the interest of any mechanical producer in this country to have the duties on his productions, or others which involve much labor, so reduced that the cheap labor of France, Belgium, Germany, and Britain can come in competition with them in our home market. And thus I fully answer the gentleman's question.

The gentleman is mistaken. I have not just discovered that there are manufactories in Cincinnati, for as I heard the gentleman pleading for a law which would inevitably check their prosperity and progress and reduce the wages of labor I thought of old Charles Cist, and wondered whether his bones were not rattling in his coffin. From almost the birth of Cincinnati he was a champion of protection, and did more than any other man to build up her workshops and manufactories, and more than twenty years ago devoted a day to conducting me through many of the largest of them.

But I want to allude further to the remarks

of the gentleman from Ohio, [Mr. STEVENSON.] Speaking of Pennsylvania, he said:

"Ah! she is shrewd! New England heretofore has had the reputation of great adroitness in taking care of her own interest, but Pennsylvania carries off the palm. Quietly she sits looking out for herself, we giving bounty, she appropriating it. And now, what is the result? If we suppose, for the sake of argument, that the tariff on iron and coal is added to the cost, then Pennsylvania received a premium on her production of iron and coal in 1868 of $14,859,168."

Has the gentleman a settled opinion on the question, Is a protective duty a tax or bounty? Or is he, like Bunsby, unable to give an opinion for want of premises on which to base it? "If so be," said Bunsby on a memorable occasion, "as he's dead, my opinion is he won't come back no more; if so be as he's alive, my opinion is he will. Do I say he will? No. Why not? Because the bearings of this observation lays in the application on it." [Laughter.] "If we suppose for the sake of argument." A teacher of political economy that has not yet made up his mind whether a protecting duty is a tax or not comes here and arraigns Pennsylvania, and holds her up to ridicule as a cormorant fattening upon public bounty or plunder. But let me go on.

Mr. STEVENSON. Will the gentleman give us his opinion upon that subject?

Mr. KELLEY. I have given it, and I will give it again.

PROTECTIVE DUTIES NOT A TAX.

Mr. Chairman, I apprehend that no enlightened student of political economy regards a protective duty as a tax. Even the gentleman from Iowa [Mr. ALLISON] admitted that in most cases it is not; yet influenced, as I think, by a clever story which the chairman of our committee, who is somewhat of a wag, tells, he does not think the principle applies to pig iron. I hope our chairman, who I see does me the honor to listen, will pardon me for referring to the anecdote. It runs thus: some years ago, during the days of the Whig party, when the chairman of the committee [Mr. SCHENCK] was here as a Representative of that party and a friend of protection, he met as a member of this House a worthy old German from Reading, Pennsylvania, a staunch Democrat, but strongly in favor of protection on iron. The gentleman from Ohio, who is fond of a joke, said to him one day, "Mr. R., I think I shall go with the free-traders on the iron sections of the tariff bill, especially on pig iron." "Why will you do that?" was the response. "Well, my people want cheap plows, nails, horseshoes, &c." "But," replied the old German, "we make iron in Pennsylvania; and if you want to keep up the supply and keep the price down you ought to encourage the manufacture." "But you know," said our chairman, "that a protective duty is a tax, and adds just that much to the cost of the article?" "Yes, I suppose it does generally increase the cost of the thing just so much as the duty is; all the leaders of our party say so, and we say so in our convention platforms

and our public meeting resolutions; but, Mr. SCHENCK, somehow or other I think it don't work just that way mit pig iron." [Laughter.]

The gentleman while admitting that protective duties do not always or even generally increase the price of the manufactured article, thinks "that somehow or other it don't work that way mit pig iron." Now, I think that iron in all its forms is subject to every general law, and that the duty of $9 per ton on pig iron has reduced the price measured in wheat, wool, and other agricultural commodities and increased the supply to such an extent as to prove that the duty has been a boon and not a tax. On nothing else produced in this country has the influence of protection been so broadly and beneficently felt by the people of the country at large.

On the 11th of January I submitted to the House some remarks in the nature of a review of the last report of Commissioner D. A. Wells, and showed that after the production of American pig iron had been without increase for a decade under the stimulus of this duty we more than doubled it in six years. The authentic figures I exhibited were as follows:

Production of pig iron in England and the United States from 1854 to 1862 inclusive.

	England.	United States.
1854	3,069,838	716,674
1855	3,218,154	754,178
1856	3,586,377	874,428
1857	3,659,447	798,157
1858	3,456,064	705,094
1859	3,712,904	840,427
1860	3,826,752	913,774
1861	3,712,390	731,564
1862	3,943,469	787,662

The Morrill tariff, which raised the duty to $6, went into effect in 1861. In 1864 the duty was raised to $9. The results have been as follows:

	England.	United States.
1863	4,510,040	947,604
1864	4,767,951	1,135,497
1865	4,819,254	931,582
1866	4,523,897	1,350,943
1867	4,761,028	1,461,626
1868	-	1,603,000
1869	-	1,900,000

In connection with these figures I then invited the attention of the House to the fact that we built last year 65 furnaces in 15 States of the Union, and that 58 more had been begun. A few years more of such wonderful progress and we will produce from our own coal and iron our entire supply of iron and steel and compete with England in supplying the demands of the world. The vast demand created by the extension of our railroad system, and those of Russia and India, are exceeding the capacity of England. She cannot largely increase her production without largely increasing its cost. The gentleman from Iowa was constrained to admit yesterday that the price of English iron has gone up steadily during the last year, because the demand is in excess of her capacity to produce; yet the price of American pig iron has fallen at least $6 per ton on all grades within the last 10 months. What is the cause of this reduction? Not British competition—and that is the only possible competition—for the price of British iron has risen. No, sir; the price of American iron has gone down under domestic competition and the general depreciation of prices. Keep your duty high enough to induce other men to build furnaces and rolling-mills and before 5 years you will find American iron cheapened to the level of the markets of the world, and that without a commensurate reduction of wages.

HOW THE INTERNAL REVENUE CAN BE DISPENSED WITH.

But I return to my subject. The gentleman from Ohio asked from what eight sources $130,000,000 of revenue can be derived. I find I overstated the number required; but six articles are necessary to give us all the income we need this year from that source. Let me state the receipts from these six sources during the last year. They were as follows:

From distilled spirits	$45,026,401
From tobacco	23,430,709
From fermented liquors	6,099,879
From banks and bankers	3,335,516
From incomes	34,791,855
From stamps	16,420,710
	$129,104,068

Sir, month by month, since the close of the last fiscal year, the receipts from each of these sources have been larger than those of the corresponding month of last year. There is a regular monthly increase in every item. Retaining but these six sources of internal revenue we can mitigate their exactions at least by increasing the exemption from the income tax or reducing the rate, and still obtain an excess over the amount that is absolutely required. I am in favor of adopting this course, and believe that in three years more, or in five at most, we can wipe out all our internal taxes except stamps and tobacco.

Mr. SCHENCK. And spirits.

Mr. KELLEY. No. I am anxious to make spirits free as soon as we can. I would make this change in the interests of the farmers of the country. But I do not wish to run into a digression, and will recur to this point. I proceed to invite the attention of the committee to the cost of collecting the internal revenue. In 1867 it was $8,982,686; in 1868, $9,327,301, and in 1869, $7,218,610, requiring for the three years the expenditure of $25,528,597. Why, sir, its abolition would be equal to the payment of $133,000,000 of the public debt. We hope to fund our interest-bearing debt at an average of 4½ per cent. This will save $18,000,000. Before the end of this fiscal year there will be in the Treasury $100,000,000 of our bonds, the interest on which is $6,000,000 per annum, which, with the other sum and the cost of collecting the internal revenue, would make a reduction of $32,500,000 in the annual expenses of the Government. If the bill under discussion shall become a law we will, I believe, although it lightens the burdens of the people at least $20,000,000 per annum, be able in five years to make even distilled spirits free, and rely on stamps and the tax on tobacco.

THE EFFECT OF PROTECTION ON PRICES AGAIN.

The gentleman from Iowa said that pig iron sells at $40 a ton and yields at least $15 profit. I have the Iron Age, a paper of the highest authority among dealers in iron and hardware, and I do not find it puts it at the price named by the gentleman. March 12 it quotes prices at Philadelphia of American pig iron, No. 1, for foundery use, as $33 50 to $34; No. 2, foundery, $31 50 to $32; gray forge, $30 to $31; white and mottled, $28 50 to $29. There is some difference between these prices and $40; and if the gentleman was as far out of the way in the profits of iron-makers as in the cost of iron he has shown clearly enough that there is no profit in making pig iron at this time. The gentleman from Ohio [Mr. GARFIELD] hands me a still later paper, showing a further reduction. But every business man knows that the price is receding under the rapid increase of domestic competition.

The English people know what would be the effect of the reduction of our duty. I hold in my hand the annual circular of a leading iron firm in London advising the English iron-makers of the state of the trade and the prospect for this year. Let me read from this circular, which I may say was evidently not intended for American consumption:

"No. 53 OLD BROAD STREET,
LONDON, December 31, 1869.

"SIR: This has been a prosperous year for the iron-masters. Our monthly advice of exports will have revealed the cause. Three countries alone—Russia, India, and the United States—have purchased 940,000 tons of British rails. Under these unprecedented exports the price has ruled firm, and good Erie rails are now worth £6 15s. net.

"Coal and pig iron.—Over-production has kept down the price; but at length the demand for pigs appears to have overtaken the supply, and they are firm at an advance of 5s. upon the year.

"Old rails have been largely used by rail-mills, and have advanced 10s. also during the year.

"Wages have advanced over the whole mining district. At a meeting in London this week the Welsh iron-masters voted an advance of 10 per cent.

"Cost of the finished rails to the manufacturer is thus settled. The buyer is, however, more interested in the relation of supply to demand.

"The supply of railway bars has greatly increased; many merchant bar-mills have taken to rails, and all the mills have increased their make. This increased product has, however, found ready sale, and will not probably decrease.

"The demand for next year promises to be good. Most of the mills have orders for three, and some for six months. Home railways must buy more largely than in 1869. India will also take more rails. Russia is not so eager a buyer as at this time last year. The Government, however, continues to build roads for commercial and military purposes, and while the English investors retain their present partiality for Russian securities there will be no lack of money. Yet with the present out-turn a material reduction of the American duty, or something equally significant, is necessary to advance the price above £7."

Yes, Mr. Chairman, a material reduction of the American duty, or something equally significant, is necessary to enable the British iron-master to advance his price beyond £7; and the day the telegraph announces that we have reduced our duty on pig and railroad iron will be the day on which the price of British iron will go up. I pray you be admonished by this circular.

I have also an article from the Manchester Examiner and Times of January 3, 1870, relating to cotton, as compared with the year preceding; and from what I shall read it will be seen that iron is not the only English interest which will be improved by the reduction of our duties. The organ of the cotton-spinners of Manchester says:

"As compared with the years preceding the American war, this country has received during the past few years £7,000,000 to £8,000,000 less per annum for the cost of manufacturing cotton, and there can be no question that in comparison with the cost of cotton this country has marketed the cheapest cloth ever made; and if cotton manufacturers on the continent of Europe had not been protected by high tariffs they would have been swept from the field."

Yes, repeal the protective duties on cotton, which are so abhorrent to the gentleman from Iowa, says the Examiner and Times of Manchester, and the free-trade league and the cotton manufactures of the country will be swept from the field.

THE TARIFFS OF ENGLAND AND FRANCE DISCRIMINATE AGAINST AMERICAN FARMERS.

The gentleman from New York [Mr. BROOKS] held up the English tariff to our view. Gentlemen may have been surprised to hear me say that I was very anxious to hasten the day when the tax on distilled spirits should be repealed. Gentlemen from the agricultural districts of France and England discriminate specially against you and your constituents in their tariffs. England derives nearly half her customs from inordinate duties on the productions of the American farmer, or from agricultural products with which this country could supply her. Let us look at the facts. The gentleman from New York held up the tariff of England; said it yields £21,602,414 sterling, or $108,000,000; but he did not invite your attention to the fact that she raises over $54,000,000, or more than one half, by duties that discriminate against our farmers. Yet such is the case. She raises from tobacco and snuff, one of our leading agricultural staples and its immediate product, £6,542,460, or $32,712,300. The friends of free trade say we do not import enough English iron; we do not import enough English cotton goods; we do not import enough English woolen goods, considering how cheap we can buy them all. If we are to reduce our duties and import more I beg the Representatives of the farming States of the West to demand something like reciprocity on behalf of their constituents, for whose grain there is no market. Every yard of cotton and woolen goods and every ton of iron represent the grain and meat consumed by the families of the men who produced it; and while our grain goes to waste for the want of purchasers, the friends of protection protest against importing that grown in other countries, even when converted into cloth or iron. The cloth and iron would be as good if made where well-paid laborers eat freely of American wheat, butter, and meat; and to those who cannot sell their crop at any price a neighboring furnace, factory, or rolling-mill would be a blessing, even though they could not buy cloth or iron at English prices. But I must proceed.

I have shown that of the $108,000,000 England raises by her tariff she gets $32,712,300 by duties on one of our agricultural staples. Her duties on tobacco are taxes, for England has no tobacco-fields to develop. They are, therefore, not protective duties. Like our duties on tea, coffee, pepper, and spice, they are taxes purely. But let us go a little further into this matter. England raises $21,667,565 on spirits. This is an absolute discrimination against our grain. Were that duty removed the farmer and distiller would be working together, and instead of exporting wheat and corn at prices that will not cover the cost of production and transportation their produce would be manufactured into alcohol, pork, and lard oil; and while our own laboring people would have cheaper provisions the farmer would greatly reduce the cost of transportation and have an ample market for his grain manufactured into alcohol, pork, and oil. Yet gentlemen representing agricultural districts plead with us to admit British goods at lower rates, while she gathers $54,599,865 in a single year by imposing such duties on tobacco as greatly diminish its consumption and such on spirits as preclude the importation of our grain in the only forms in which it can be profitably exported.

ENGLAND A HIDEOUS MONOPOLY—FREE TRADE SUPPORTS IT.

Mr. BROOKS, of New York. Let me state that our great agricultural products—cotton, which is an immense product, and wheat, corn, &c.—are admitted duty free.

Mr. KELLEY. To that I reply that they take our cotton because they cannot live without it, and our wheat and corn when they cannot buy cereals cheaper elsewhere. France has a duty on wheat and flour even when imported in French vessels. We are too far from the sea-board, and the cost of transportation from our grain-fields is too great for us to send them grain in bulk at present prices. The cheapest way of transporting corn is in the form of alcohol. In this form we could send it profitably were their duties not prohibitory. England will take raw materials from countries from which she can buy cheapest. But her much-lauded free trade does not offer any advantage to the American. Gentlemen talk about monopolists, and aver that protection fosters monopolies. Sir, the world has never seen, so heartless, so unrelenting, and so gigantic a monopoly as the British Government and the manufacturing power that sustains it. It is a monopoly which has desolated Ireland and swept her factories from the face of the earth. Ireland, less than a century ago, before the union, the home of a contented people, and, the seat of a busy and prosperous industry, is now a land whose people are born only to be watched and hunted as felons, or exiled from the land they love so well. The manufacturing and landed monopoly of England but a few years ago huddled into their graves the decaying bodies of more than 1,000,000 of the people of Ireland, who died of starvation in a single year.

It is a monopoly which has inflicted on British India wrongs even greater than these. Three years ago the air of the whole wide district of Orissa was fetid with the stench rising from the decaying bodies of more than 1,000,000 people who had starved in one of the richest agricultural regions in the world, because under England's enlightened free trade they were not permitted to diversify their industries, and when their single crop failed they were permitted to starve, as the Irish were when the rot assailed their only crop, the potato. This English monopoly is so absolute and selfish that it will not allow provinces and colonies to diversify their industry. It binds them to the culture of one product—India, cotton, and Ireland, men for exportation. Shall she also hold the people of the Northwest as her commercial subjects and doom them to raise wheat and wheat alone? We can break its power and overthrow this monstrous monopoly. Yes, by peaceful arts, without the clash of arms, we can emancipate the hundreds of millions of people England now oppresses. The source of her power is her commercial and manufacturing supremacy, and this we can and should undermine, as we are its chief support. With our cotton-fields, our widespread and inexhaustible deposits of all the metals, and our immense sheep-walks, we should supply all our wants. When we do this our commerce will revive, for populous nations that supply their own markets always produce a surplus which they can export at low prices. But now England properly regards us as a dependency more profitable than "all the English-speaking dependencies of the empire." On this point the London Times of February 25, when discussing the bill now under consideration, says:

"The fiscal policy of the United States is for us a subject of no remote or transient interest. Although statistics may be adduced to prove that in proportion to population the colonies are our best customers, yet in the mass our trade with republican America is by far the largest item in the balance-sheet of our exports to foreign countries, and is nearly equal to that with all the English-speaking dependencies of the empire."

A HOME MARKET—A PREDICTION FULFILLED.

Gentlemen sneer at the idea of a home market. Sir, on the 1st of June, 1868, we had under consideration a proposition to permit table whisky to remain in bond under certain conditions. In the course of the discussion I urged upon gentlemen from the West who were opposing it the propriety of giving effect to that proposition. I pressed upon the attention of the House the fact that age quadrupled the value by improving the quality of fine whisky, and that our whisky was superseding French brandy in general use. I urged the importance of this to the grain-growing States. Turning to my remarks I find the following prediction, the fulfillment of which has occurred even before I expected it:

"The people of the Northwest, it seems to me, are specially interested in this question. They will find that they cannot afford to expel from their inland section of the country any branch of manufactures. They need the opportunity to export their grain concentrated in the form of whisky, high-wines, or other manufactures. I am no Cassandra and they will not believe me, but I tell them they are entering upon a competition that will exclude them from the markets of the world if they depend upon the export of their grain in bulk as food or mere raw material. Do you mark, gentlemen of Missouri, Illinois, and Wisconsin, that California is loud in the expression of her gratitude for the fact that 130 vessels have been added to the fleet for carrying her grain to New York and trans-atlantic ports? They can send grain in bulk 23,000 miles to the sea-board of New England or Old England at less cost for transportation than you can send yours to the sea-board by rail. Oregon is groaning under her crop of wheat, and her people are fearing that means of its transportation to market may not be at hand. But this distant competition is not what you have most cause to dread. The South, no longer your customer for food for man and beast, looms up your competitor. Her advantages over you are manifold as they are manifest. She lies between you and the ocean. Her grain-fields are upon the banks of navigable rivers which flow to the Gulf or the ocean, and at or near the mouth of each is a sea-port. From Norfolk around to Galveston, Texas, the grain of the farmers of the several States may be floated to the sea-board upon rafts and there find shipping. England and western Europe are not the countries to which we chiefly export grain and flour. Our chief markets for these are Central and South America, and the islands to which the southern States are neighbors; and I tell you that if the people of the far Northwest do not take heed, and by diversifying their industry convert their raw materials into more compact productions, the day is not three years distant when their crops will waste in the fields for the want of a market to which they will pay the cost of transportation."

Not two years have gone by, and you are crying out that you have raised wheat in vain, that there is no market for it; that the cost of getting it to a market consumes it. Ay, and the gentleman from Iowa [Mr. ALLISON] says that in the face of these facts we are offering inducements to thousands to go at wheat-growing, that the homestead law is tempting immigrants to engage in wheat-growing and add to the unsalable and unavailable stock. That is true; and how would he improve matters? He agrees with me that the homestead law is beneficent and should not be repealed. What, then, is the gentleman's proposition. It is identical with those we have heard from so many gentlemen—reduced duties on coal, salt, hides, lumber, iron, and woolen goods. This is the burden and refrain of all the sweet singers trained in the musical academy of D. A. Wells, Commissioner of Revenue, and let us right here test its merit. Lower the duties on coal, salt, lumber, hides, iron, and woolen goods. Well, how will this increase the number of consumers of American grain or diminish the number of grain-growers? There are more than 1,500,000 of our people engaged in or dependent on the labor of producing these articles. What will become of them? They cannot live on "rye and potatoes," as German workmen in the same trades do. They will not even be content to get meat once a week, as the workmen of England are; and if they be not work must stop. And I ask gentlemen from the grain country what they suppose these people will do with themselves when the fire has gone out in the forge and furnace, and the loom and spindle stand still, and the salt-kettle rusts, and there is no work in the coal mine because the manufactures that made a market for it have been transferred to foreign countries in which wages are low and where the "working people live on rye and potatoes."

Thank God, we cannot doom them to this fate. The homestead law is their protection. In a cabin on 120 acres of public land they can raise wheat, potatoes, and a few sheep and pigs; the old-fashioned spinning-wheel and loom, easily made by skilled mechanics, will convert their home-grown wool into fabrics, and they can thus live till wiser legislators succeed us and reanimate the general industries of the country by restoring the protective system now in force.

Is that the remedy? Is free trade a specific for all or any of our ills? No, sir, it is sheer quackery, charlatanism. The only cure, the evil of which western grain-growers complain, is to increase the number of consumers and decrease the number of growers of wheat; raise, if possible, the wages of workmen so as to make mechanical employments attractive; say to the farmers' sons, "There is work and good wages for you in the machine-shop, the forge, the furnace, or the mill;" say to them whose capital is unproductive on farms, "Build mills, sink shafts to the coal-bed which underlies your farm; avail yourselves of the limestone quarry and the ore-bed, whether of iron, lead, copper, zinc, or nickel; employ your industry and capital so that it shall be profitable to you, your country, and mankind;" and in a little while you will cheapen iron and steel and make an adequate market for all the grain of the country. The gentleman's remedy is the theory of the homeopathic physician, that like cures like, which though it may be correct in physics, is not an approved maxim in social science.

Mr. ALLISON. I would like the gentleman to state how long it will be before that happy period will arrive?

Mr. KELLEY. Well, sir, I cannot tell exactly. It will depend upon the degree of promptness with which the remedy is applied. But if the Clerk will do me the kindness to give me a little rest by reading a letter from an Irish patriot, one who knew England's tenderness for her laboring people experimentally at home in Ireland, and who laid one of his limbs away in the service of our country during the war, and now lives in Quincy, Illinois, I will endeavor to give the gentleman some idea.

The Clerk read as follows:

"We have a population of 35,000 or 40,000, and our citizens are just commencing to awake to the necessity of encouraging local manufacturing. We have 2 paper mills, 10 flour mills, 5 tobacco factories; sales $1,300,000; 9 machine-shops; sales $1,050,000; 5 machine founderies; 4 stove founderies turned out last year 36,400 stoves, amounting to $473,200 cash sales; 2 boilershops, turning out $216,000 per year; 15 wagon and plow shops, with a capital of $260,000; 4 planing mills, capital $180,000; 14 manufacturers of saddles and harness, capital $233,400; and numerous others too tedious to mention. There is a company at present engaged in boring for coal, with fine prospects of success. If we can only get coal here manufacturing will spring up all around us. I have thought some of organizing a stock company to build factories and supply funds to encourage skilled workmen to enter into what is called the coöperative system. I shall shortly test the matter to see if it can be made to work.

"If the friends of protection can hold their own till after the taking of the census the crisis will be passed, for that will show such progress in the material wealth of the nation that it will require a bold man indeed to attack our system of labor. It is useless for us to talk of competing with England while she keeps as many of her people in her poor-houses as she does in her public schools—a country that expends seven eighths more to keep up her poor-houses than she does to support her schools. England and Scotland have a population of 24,599,277, for the education of which she has 14,591 schools, with 12,832 teachers, costing annually $4,212,500, while she expends for her poor-houses annually $32,595,000. Compare her with Illinois, a State sixty years ago in possession of the savages, but now possessing a population of about 2,500,000, with 11,000 schools and 20,000 teachers, costing $6,500,000 annually, more than 50 per cent. greater than England, with a population ten times larger than us. The free-trader says that pauperism is growing less in England under her free-trade system; but I find, from Purdy's Report in 1866, she had 842,860; and I see by the American Cyclopedia of 1863 for that year 1,034,832 paupers are reported. These are facts for the American people to profit by. It is reported that there are now in London more than 80,000 skilled workmen out of employment. We hear much about English liberty, but I have been of the opinion that the kind of liberty they are enjoying is that the wolf accords the lamb or the strong toward the weak in all nations—a liberty which, I trust, will never find a place among our institutions.

"The sympathizers or advocates of this English system say that free trade will give us a market for our surplus produce in Europe. But I find the more we ship the less we receive. In 1868 we exported to England 4,414,230 hundred weight of wheat, receiving therefor $17,952,850; in 1869, for the same period, 7,938,818 hundred weight, receiving therefrom only $17,740,770, or $211,000 less than we received for half the amount the previous year. If we were to change our policy, and instead of sending our wheat to England induce those 80,000 skilled workmen to come to us we would not then be compelled to look to England for a market. They will be compelled to come to us for our cotton and tobacco; but there is no need of us going to them for manufactured goods. We can take their surplus labor, transfer it to this country, and ultimately tend to the welfare of both, and thereby accomplish more than the sentimental philanthropists of Europe and America can ever do by preaching "free trade." We are influenced too much by the political economists of Europe, who write to tickle the fancy of the wealthy few, without any regard to the rights of the laboring millions."

Mr. KELLEY. I desire in this connection, and before turning to other topics, to present a brief extract from a speech made in the United States Senate by the experienced merchant and enlightened statesman who represents New Jersey in that body, Hon. ALEXANDER G. CATTELL. In the course of his remarks on the 22d of January, 1867, he said:

"But, Mr. President, the harmony of interests which exists between agriculture and manufactures, and the truth of the position I have taken, are clearly shown by actual results. I am sure the Senate will excuse me if I draw an illustration from personal observation in my own mercantile life. Twenty years ago last autumn I embarked in the trade in breadstuffs in the city of Philadelphia. At that time, and for some succeeding years, the entire volume of my business was made up of consignments of agricultural products from the valleys of the Susquehanna, the Juniata, and the Lehigh. I have not the figures at command, but I am sure I speak within bounds when I say that my own house and the four or five others doing business from the same points must have received from this quarter 4,000,000 to 5,000,000 bushels of cereals per annum. Philadelphia is still the natural market for the surplus product of this territory, but for some years past there have not been consignments enough received from that entire section to realize commissions sufficient to pay the salary of a receiving clerk.

"Do you ask, has production fallen off? I answer, no; on the contrary, it has increased, but the whole line of these valleys has been dotted with furnaces and forges and rolling-mills and saw-mills and factories and workshops, filled with operatives, and the consumer of agricultural products has been brought to the farmer's doors. He now finds a readier market for his products at home at prices equal to those ruling on the sea-board, of which he avails himself and thus saves all the cost of transportation and factorage, equal at average prices to about 20 per cent. Nay, more, sir, my own firm has frequently within the past few years sold and shipped to the millers in one of these valleys, that in which the iron interest has been most developed, the Lehigh, wheat drawn from Michigan, Illinois, Wisconsin, and Iowa to supply the deficiency in the consumptive want. And these products of the prairies of the West were sold, too, at a price far in excess of what could have been realized by exportation to any country on the face of the globe. As a consequence of this state of things land has risen in value through all this section, and farms that could have been bought fifteen or twenty years ago at $40 or $50 per acre are now salable at $150 or $200 per acre. Villages have grown to be towns, and towns have grown to be cities, agriculture and manufactures have clasped hands and prosperity reigns."

PROTECTION STIMULATES IMMIGRATION.

Sir, the gentleman from Iowa asked how long it would take if we shut up our machine-shops and mills, and closed our coal-mines, to turn 100,000 men into agriculturists. It would take one season.

Mr. ALLISON. Oh no; that was not my question.

Mr. KELLEY. That was what I was stating when you interrupted me.

Mr. ALLISON. I wanted to know how long it would be before iron and steel would be produced at a cheaper rate than it is now imported. That was my question.

Mr. KELLEY. I do not think I said cheaper than it is now imported, but cheaper than it can then be imported. As the price goes down here it is going up in England; and under the present duty we will soon be able to supply our own demand, and meet England in common markets at equal prices. Sir, I want to show gentlemen from the West what effect the tariff has on immigration. I have before me the tariffs from the organization of the Government down to the present time, given in *ad valorem* percentages, and a statement of the number of immigrants that arrived in each year, from 1856 to 1869 inclusive. By comparing them I find that whenever our duties have been low immigration fell off, and whenever our duties have been high the volume of

immigration increased. This seems to be a fixed law.

Both papers are taken from the immaculate report of David A. Wells, Special Commissioner of Internal Revenue, and I therefore present them with some hesitancy, and with the remark that if they are incorrect it is not my fault.

I find by these tables that in the nine years from 1856 to 1864, inclusive, we received 1,403,497 immigrants; and in the four years of the protective tariff, of which so many gentlemen from the West whose States are not overcrowded complain, we have received 1,514,816, or over 111,000 more in the four years of pretection than in the nine preceding years of free trade and low tariff. But I had better let the statement speak for itself. In introducing it Mr. Wells says:

"The following is a revised and the most accurate attainable statement of the course of alien immigration into the United States since and including the year 1856:

1856	200,436
1857	251,300
1858	123,126
1859	121,282
1860	153,640
1861	91,920
1862	91,987
1863	176,282
1864	193,418
1865	248,120
1866	318,554
1867	298,358
1868	297,215
1869	352,569
Total in fourteen years	2,918,213

"Total from July 1, 1865, to June 30, 1869, five years, 1,514,816."

In 1856 the rate of duty on the aggregate of our imports was 20.3, and the number of immigrants were 200,436 ; in 1859 the rate of duties had been reduced to 14.6, and the number of immigrants fell to 121,282. In 1861, by the acts of March 2, August 5, and December 24 the rate of duties was further reduced to 11.2. This broke the camel's back. So many men were thrown out of employment and wages sunk so low that none but agriculturists could come to us with any prospect of improving their condition, and immigration sunk to a point lower than it had been since the ever-to-be-remembered free-trade crisis of 1837-40. In that year but 91,920 immigrants arrived, and the depression continued through the next year and the number of immigrants was but 91,987. By the act of July 14, 1862 the duties were raised, so that in 1863 they were up to 23.7, and the immigration nearly equaled that of the two preceding years, having gone up 176,282. By the several acts of 1864, 1865, and 1866 the duties were increased, so that the duties on the importations of 1866 averaged 40.2 per cent., and immigration went up to 318,554. Last year, when the West was further oppressed by the increase of duties on wool and copper, they averaged 41.2, and the number of immigrants went up to 352,569 ; and the commissioners of immigration assure us that this year the number will exceed 400,000.

It is thus demonstrated historically that previously as we make our duties protective of high ... for labor, so do we bring skilled work-... from Germany, Belgium, France, and ... to work in our mines, forges, fur-..., rolling-mills, cotton and woolen facto-..., and create a home market for the grain of Iowa, Illinois, and the other States whose farmers complain that they have no market for their grain.

SKILLED WORKMEN THE MOST VALUABLE COMMODITY WE CAN IMPORT.

Mr. SCHENCK. We have free trade in men.

Mr. KELLEY. The chairman of the Committee of Ways and Means [Mr. SCHENCK] suggests in this connection that we have free trade in men. Yes, men are on the free list. They cost us not even freight. Yet how they swell the revenues and help us pay the debt of the country! They are raised from helpless infancy, through tender childhood, and trained to skilled labor in youth in other lands, and in manhood allured by higher wages, they come to us and are welcomed to citizenship. In this way we have maintained a balance of trade that has enabled us to resist without bankruptcy the ordinary commercial balance that has been so heavily against us. We promote free trade in men, and it is the only free trade I am prepared to promote.

FRENCH FREE TRADE.

The French tariff is as inimical to us as that of England. It is replete with prohibitory duties and absolute prohibitions. Yet France is spoken of to us by the English journals and in the declamations of gentlemen as a free-trade nation. Why, sir, on every article mentioned in the French tariff, unless it is absolutely free, the duty is so much if imported in French vessels, and so much more if imported in vessels of other nations. Every head of a column of the rates of duty established by the French tariff shows that you cannot import dutiable articles into France at the same rate in the vessel of another nation that you can in a French one. They read thus:

Articles.	General tariff.		Import tariff in treaty with Great Britain and other countries.	
	Imports.			
	In French vessels.	In other vessels.	In French and treaty vessels.	In other vessels.

Mr. ALLISON. Are you in favor of that rule?

Mr. KELLEY. I am.

Mr. ALLISON. So am I.

Mr. KELLEY. I am in favor of imposing duties so as to discriminate in favor of American shipping. I am for every form of protection to American industry and enterprise.

In the French tariff tobacco is classed as a colonial product, and its importation on private account is prohibited. It is a Government monopoly. American grown tobacco, even in the leaf, is admitted into France only when the colonial supply fails; and then if it is carried in other than a French vessel it is made to pay a duty of nearly 1 cent on the pound, which is imposed in order to tax foreign shipping.

The gentleman from Iowa objects to the schedule under which duties are to be assessed under the committee's bill, and specially to that of sugar. Let me invite his attention to some of the provisions of the French tariff on sugar: sugar from other than French possessions; sugar similar to refined powdered, above No. 20, from foreign countries, &c.; sugar, refined, from other possessions, are prohibited. Thus all sugars refined or advanced in other than French possessions are prohibited, as is also molasses.

Mr. SCHENCK. That has built up their beet-sugar manufacture.

Mr. KELLEY. Yes; and it is an industry we should build up in the West. I want to run cursorily through this tariff. The importation of cast iron into France is prohibited. Wrought iron in plates is prohibited. Manufactures of iron of certain kinds are prohibited. All chemical products not enumerated are prohibited. All extracts of dye-woods are prohibited. Dye-woods are admitted free; but if American or other labor has been expended in making extracts from dye-woods the extracts are prohibited. Gentlemen of the free-trade school generally and the gentlemen from New York [Mr. BROOKS] and from Iowa [Mr. ALLISON] assail vehemently, and as I think most unfairly, the iron schedule and duties on steel proposed by the committee's bill. How differently France estimates the importance of these vital industries. Her tariff prohibits all manufactures of zinc and other metals not specially named and the following articles of iron and steel, in the production of which we excel both her and England in quality and cheapness:

"Castings, not polished: chairs for railroads, plates, &c., cast in open air; cylindric tubes, plain or grooved columns, gas-retorts, &c., and other articles without ornament or finish; hollow-ware not included above; castings, polished or turned: the same, tinned, varnished, &c.; household utensils and other articles not enumerated, of iron or sheet iron, polished or painted; same, enameled or varnished; all articles of steel; iron, blacksmiths' work; locksmiths' work; nails, by machine: nails, by hand; wood-screws, bolts, screw-nuts."

France prohibits and excludes these articles that her poorly paid workmen may be protected against the productions of those of Belgium and Germany, who receive even less than they. All tissues of cotton, except nankeens, produce of India, lace, manufactured by hand or otherwise, and tulle, with lace-work, are also prohibited. Cotton and woolen yarns are also prohibited by the general tariff, though admitted at high and most scientifically rated protective duties from England under the import tariff treaty with that country.

Yes, sir, if we spin our cotton into yarn, or weave it into a tissue or fabric, it is excluded from the broad empire of France. If you carry it there raw, with no labor in it save that of the slave or the freedman, you can take it in, but as yarn or a tissue it is prohibited.

THE PURPOSE OF THE FREE LIST.

The committee in proposing the extended free list embraced in the second section of the bill hoped to accomplish two important objects, one of which was to promote direct commerce between us and those non-manufacturing countries which require the productions of our shops and mills, and whose raw materials we require; and the other was to give our manufacturers and mechanics, free of duty, those essentials which France, England, and Belgium admit free. A majority of the committee believe that the adoption of this will do much to revive our commerce, and not only quicken established industries, but lead to the introduction of new ones, and thus increase the market for the productions of the farm and reduce the cost and price of a large range of manufactured goods. We think it is sound policy to let in free raw materials that we cannot produce, and collect our revenue from articles in the production of which labor has been expended. This is the theory of the bill we reported. It has the sanction of the sagacity and experience of France and England, and was framed regardless of the teachings of mere theorists and school-men.

DUTIES ON WOOL AND WOOLENS.

Mr. Chairman, although I had made some preparation for its illustration, I had not expected to go into so general a discussion of the effect of protection upon the interests of the farmer. The wide range the discussion has taken must be my apology for one other view of the subject. The gentleman from Iowa told us that the wool interest is suffering from the excessive duties imposed on woolen cloths by the existing tariff, and that the committee proposes to continue them. Sir, I may be very dull, but after hearing the gentleman it still seems to me that the wool interest must have been benefited by the bill increasing the duties on wool and woolens. We certainly have more people wearing wool now than we had in 1860. We have, as I have shown, received over 2,000,000 immigrants since then, and our natural increase is at least 1,000,000 per annum; yet I find by the thirteenth report of the commissioners of her Britannic Majesty's customs that the declared value of woolen manufactures exported to the United States was, in June, 1860, £3,414,050, while in 1868, nearly a decade thereafter, it was £3,658,432—an increase of £234,382 in 8 years.

Who has grown the wool that clothes our increased population? Our freedmen now wear ordinary woolen clothes. The "poor whites" of the South now wear what they call "store goods," but to which they were unused before the rebellion. The cold Northwest, whose

people wear woolen goods all the year, has increased its population so largely that it is demanding enlarged representation on this floor without waiting for the census.

Our wool-wearing population has nearly doubled; yet the amount of wool imported is scarcely greater than it was eight years ago. Where does the wool come from? Does it drop gently from the heavens, like the dew, or is it grown upon the sheep of western and southern farmers?

THE WAY TO REDUCE THE TAXES.

Sir, I am as anxious to reduce taxes as rapidly as it can be done consistently with the maintenance of the public credit and the gradual extinguishment of the debt as any man on this floor. I do not make this declaration now for the first time. On the 31st of January, 1866, I saw that, the war being over, the freedmen must be provided with the means of making a living by other labor than that of the plantation hand; that the women of the South must have employment; that there must be a diversification of our industry; that the Northwest would be shut out from her markets if she did not diversify her industry; and in the course of some remarks I made that day in favor of remitting taxes, both internal and external, I described the bill now under consideration. In stating how I would reduce the burdens of the people I said:

"I have never been able to believe that a national debt is a national blessing. I have seen how good might be interwoven with or educed from evil, or how a great evil might, under certain conditions, be turned to good account; but beyond this I have never been able to regard debt, individual or national, as a blessing. It may be that, as in the inscrutable providence of God it required nearly five years of war to extirpate the national crime of slavery, and anguish and grief found their way to nearly every hearth-side in the country before we would recognize the manhood of the race we had so long oppressed, it was also necessary that we should be involved in a debt of unparalleled magnitude that we might be compelled to avail ourselves of the wealth that lies so freely around us, and by opening markets for well-rewarded industry make our land, what in theory it has ever been, the refuge of the oppressed of all climes. England, if supreme selfishness be consistent with sagacity, has been eminently sagacious in preventing us from becoming a manufacturing people; forwith our enterprise, our ingenuity, our freer institutions, the extent of our country, the cheapness of our land, the diversity of our resources, the grandeur of our seas, lakes, and rivers, we should long ago have been able to offer her best workmen such inducements as would have brought them by millions to help bear our burdens and fight our battles. We can thus raise the standard of British and continental wages and protect American workmen against ill-paid competition. This we must do if we mean to maintain the national honor. The fields now under culture, the houses now existing, the mines now being worked, the men we now employ, cannot pay our debt. To meet its annual interest by taxing our present population and developed resources would be to continue an ever-enduring burden.

"The principal of the debt must be paid; but as it was contracted for posterity its extinguishment should not impoverish those who sustained the burdens of the war. I am not anxious to reduce the total of our debt, and would in this respect follow the example of England, and as its amount has been fixed would not for the present trouble myself about its aggregate except to prevent its increase. My anxiety is that the taxes it involves shall be as little oppressive as possible, and be so adjusted that while *defending our industry against foreign assault, they may add nothing to the cost of those necessaries of life which we cannot produce, and for which we must therefore look to other lands. The raw materials entering into our manufactures, which we are yet unable to produce, but on which we unwisely impose duties, I would put into the free list with tea, coffee, and other such purely foreign essentials of life, and would impose duties on commodities that compete with American productions, so as to protect every feeble or infant branch of industry and quicken those that are robust. I would thus cheapen the elements of life and enable those whose capital is embarked in any branch of production to offer such wages to the skilled workmen of all lands as would steadily and rapidly increase our numbers, and, as is always the case in the neighborhood of growing cities or towns of considerable extent, increase the return for farm labor; this policy would open new mines and quarries, build new furnaces, forges, and factories, and rapidly increase the taxable property and taxable inhabitants of the country.*

"Let us pursue for twenty years the sound national policy of protection, and we will double our population and more than quadruple our capital and reduce our indebtedness per capita and per acre to little more than a nominal sum. Thus each man can 'without moneys' pay the bulk of his portion of the debt by blessing others with the ability to bear an honorable burden."

My views on these points have undergone no change, and I cannot more aptly describe the bill before the committee, in general terms, than I thus did more than four years ago.

THE DEFECTS OF THE PRESENT TARIFF AND THE REMEDIES SUGGESTED BY THE NEW BILL.

Why not maintain the existing tariff, and wherein does the bill submitted by the Committee of Ways and Means differ from it? Several gentlemen have propounded these questions, and I now propose to answer them briefly and rapidly. The existing law is crude and contains many incongruous provisions. It is not in accord with the theory of the free-trader or the protectionist. It imposes the heaviest duties on articles of common consumption that we cannot produce. Thus, on chalk, not an inch of which has, so far as I have heard, been discovered in our country, it imposes a duty of 833⅓ per cent. It is bought at from 75 cents to $1 50 per ton, and the duty is $10. This onerous duty is not protective. We have no chalk-fields, and produce no substitute for it. It is therefore simply a tax, and one that everybody feels; the boy at his game of marbles, or before the blackboard in school, the housewife when she cleans her silver or britannia ware, and the farmer in the cost of putty for his windows. The new bill puts chalk on the free list.

Mr. ALLISON. Have we not increased the duty on putty, which enters into use in the house of every citizen in the land?

Mr. KELLEY. Yes, sir; and why did we do it? All our western farmers are raising wheat, and many of them can find no market for their crop, and this bill, it is hoped, will, if it become a law, induce some of them to produce other things. We import immense amounts of linseed and castor-oil, and the majority of the committee hoped that by raising the duty on these oils, and those which may be substituted for them, it would induce some of them to raise flax and manufacture the oil. Again, we import great quantities of goods made of flax and substitutes for it, and we hoped that better duties on the oil and on these fabrics might lead to the establishment of linen and other mills in the interior. And as linseed-oil is the ingredient of chief value in putty, we raised the duty on it to correspond with that on oil. We hope thus to secure to every citizen good and cheap putty, made of free chalk and American-grown oil.

THE ALLEGATION THAT WE PROTECT OUR MANUFACTURES BY DUTIES AVERAGING FORTY PER CENT. IS NOT TRUE.

Mr. Chairman, I desire to call attention to the unfairness, unintentional of course, of the statement of the gentleman from New York [Mr. BROOKS] that the existing tariff gives protection equal to an average of 41.2 per cent. That is the percentage of duties on the aggregate of our imports, and he will hardly claim that the duty of over 833 per cent. on chalk is protective of any of our industries.

Again, we collect a duty of 300 per cent. on pepper. Why should black pepper pay 300 per cent.? Do we grow it anywhere in this country? Is this duty protective of any of our industries? You pay 5 cents a pound for pepper and the tariff imposes a duty of 15 cents, gold, equal to 300 per cent., and the gentleman includes this in his average of protective duties. Do we grow cloves or clove-stems in any part of the country? Is the duty on them protective? It is on cloves 355 per cent. and on clove-stems 386 per cent., and yet the gentleman also includes these with his protective duties. I think gentlemen perceive by this time what I meant when I said that many of the provisions of the present tariff are incongruous. While many of them are high enough for protection they are countervailed by higher duties on raw materials that we cannot produce, and which rival nations admit free or under very low duties.

I shall not attempt to bring all such incongruities to the attention of the committee, but beg leave to allude to a few more. On cayenne pepper, the duty is 303 per cent.; on allspice, 376¼ per cent.; on nutmegs, 188½ per cent.; on crude camphor, 113 per cent.; on saltpeter, 77¾ per cent.; on varnish gums, none of which are produced in this country, 80 per cent.; on tea, the laborer's refreshing drink, 78½ per cent.; on coffee, 47½ per cent. I could largely extend this list of duties, each of which is a tax on some article of common consumption not produced in the country, and to that extent a bonus to our competitors. I am in favor of making all such articles free; and the committee has reduced the duties on them or put them on the free list. When this shall be done the gentleman from New York can calculate the percentage and find that our duties will compare favorably with those imposed by England and France.

DUTIES WHICH NEED READJUSTMENT.

Another serious fault of the existing law is that so many of its duties are *ad valorem*. Dishonest men take advantage of this and have goods invoiced below the proper value, and thus not only defraud the Government, but do wrong to both the home manufacturer and the honest importer. This system of duties has much to do with the decline of American commerce. The large temptation to defraud the Government by undervaluation has caused great houses abroad to establish agencies here and to refuse to sell directly to an American purchaser. This is so with all the Sheffield steel-makers and most of the continental silk houses. In this way the frauds of the steel-makers and silk manufacturers have been enormous, amounting to many millions of dollars. The new bill substitutes specific duties wherever it is practicable.

The duties now collected on alcoholic preparations, and those in the production of which spirits are used, such as quinine, chloroform, collodion, &c., are now much too high, having been adjusted to the tax of $2 per gallon on distilled spirits. The new bill adjusts them to the lower tax now collected.

Many of the existing duties are so high as to defeat all their legitimate objects and deprive the Government of all revenue. This is especially true of spices. It was in evidence from many sources that these are imported into New York or San Francisco and immediately shipped in bond to the British provinces, whence they are smuggled back. The bill of the committee proposes such reductions of the duties as will probably give the Government a handsome revenue while cheapening them to the consumer. The value to the country of the changes proposed cannot fail to be very great.

THE PRESENT LAW SHOULD BE REVISED, NOT OVER-
THROWN.

Would that I could impress upon the House my estimate of the value to the country of these changes. I am discussing the bill in no spirit of partisanship. In urging its acceptance I am pleading the cause of the farmer and laborer, as I conscientiously believe that it will, if adopted, increase the purchasing power, the exchangeable value of every bushel of grain grown and hour of labor performed in our country. I have no general condemnation for the existing law. It needs revision, but should not be overthrown. As a revenue measure it has exceeded the anticipations of its friends and the most earnest friends of the Government. It yielded for the year ending June 30, 1867, $176,417,810; for the year ending June 30, 1868, $164,464,599 56; and for the year ending June 30, 1869, $180,084,456 63; and no preceding tariff produced results comparable to these.

And, sir, notwithstanding these faults it has been of great value as a protective measure. By its protective influence it has added much to the power of the country and the prosperity of the people. Under it our production of pig iron has been more than doubled, as I have already shown, and its production has been extended into new and large fields in States where it was previously unknown. increased value been given to all the lands States; the increase being equal to of the value of the mineral lands the agricultural surface; and it has provided a market in the of each furnace, in which articles which would not bear transportation points or foreign lands. The and Minnesota now produce for anything else than wheat and wool ation to the sea-board States or When manufactories are built at mines villages spring up and create a market as potatoes and turnips, the produce garden and the orchard, and for hay, the western farmer will be relieved necessity of growing successive crops to the exhaustion of the soil. They also afford a market for lamb, veal, all the thousand things that come of iary sources of income even to those on a great scale. Thus have many the protective influence of the as well as in the stimulus it has given migration, and the addition of the the agricultural value of immense land in almost every State; and while endeavor ing to improve it I renew my protest against its repeal or overthrow.

THE CAREFUL CONSIDERATION THAT WAS BE
STOWED UPON THE BILL BY THE COMMITTEE

Mr. Chairman and gentlemen of the commit tee, your Committee of Ways and Means devoted the earnest labor of a year to the con sideration of the revision of the tariff, as you committed to them by special resolution of the House. In the discharge of that duty we have traveled in great part at our own per sonal cost, relieved largely by the hospitality of rail road, steamship, and other transportation com panies, from the rocky coasts of Massachu setts, and the waters of its bay, along the coast of California and Oregon, and over the beautiful waters of Puget sound, the Willa mette and the Columbia rivers; we have list ened to merchants, manufacturers, farmers, and men of enterprise, representing all the interests of every section of the country; and we have been in all respects painstaking and deliberate in our efforts to ascertain how the existing pro visions of the tariff can be so modified as to yield the Government adequate revenue, lighten the bur dens of the people, and stimulate all the in dustries with equal hand. And I conscientiously believe that if the bill we have reported shall be adopted without an amendment, as those the committee is prepared to suggest, the quickening influence would be felt in every department of the productive and commercial industries of the country. It would do much to revivify the languishing shipping interest It would give new and grander proportions to the market for your agricultural products. It would maintain in a healthy condition your manu facturing and mechanical establishments, and it would say to capitalists here and abroad

"The protective policy of the country is confirmed; you may safely embark in new enterprises and develop new elements of the illimitable store and varieties of wealth now lying dormant within the country."

HOW IT WILL STIMULATE THE SHIPPING INTEREST.

Do gentlemen ask how it will quicken commerce? Let them turn to its free list. Our commerce is now with manufacturing nations inhabiting the grain-growing and metalliferous regions of Europe. They produce everything we do except cotton, rice, tobacco, and petroleum; other than these they want but little from us, unless war or drought or excessive rain prevails over so large a section as to materially diminish the grain crop. We should cultivate an exchange of products with the non-manufacturing tropical or semi-tropical countries. We want their gums, spices, barks, ivory, dye-woods, drugs, and other productions which they would gladly exchange for our grain, spirits, cotton fabrics, axes, hoes, shovels, and an infinite variety of our productions. These countries are our natural markets, but we have excluded ourselves from them by our tariff laws. All other manufacturing countries admit their productions free, while we impose duties on them which, as I have shown, are taxes upon ourselves in their consumption. But this does a further wrong to the shipping interest in this wise: the London merchant gets their production in exchange for the shoddy cloth, low-grade iron, and general "Brumanagen" wares of England, and imports them free of duty. He ships them to us in English steamers, and adds freight to his many other profits. This trade of right belongs to us, and under the committee's bill we will enjoy it.

Let me illustrate by a single example. The cost of saltpeter is a question of importance to every railroad builder, quarryman, and miner, and we ought to import the raw material from two countries remote from each other and manufacture it more cheaply than we now import it through London from India. The duties on this article are higher than they should be, and so apportioned as to discriminate against our labor. That on the crude article is 25 per cent. higher than that on the partially refined, and is at the rate of 77¾ per cent. They are as follows: on partially refined saltpeter, 2 cents per pound; on crude, 2½ cents, and on refined, 3 cents. The new bill removes the discrimination against ourselves and makes but two grades of duty. It reduces that on the crude article to 1½ cent, and on the refined to 2½ cents. But while thus reducing the duty on this important article the bill of the committee invites the establishment of its cheaper manufacture in our midst and the employment of many ships in bringing us the raw material in equal proportions from Peru and Germany.

If gentlemen will examine the free list they will find that it embraces muriate of potassa and nitrate of soda. The latter is a natural product of Peru, and the former of Germany, and from 1,000 tons of each we can produce 1,000 tons of saltpeter cheaper than we can import it from India. This would double the tonnage required for the carrying of this article. I have thus presented to the committee but one of many illustrations with which I might detain them of the influence the bill will exercise upon our commerce if it becomes a law.

STEEL AD VALOREM.

I have said that one of the defects of the present law is its frequent application of *ad valorems*, which open the door to great frauds. I turn for an illustration to what seems to be a favorite topic of the gentleman from Iowa, [Mr. ALLISON]—the article of steel. The gentleman said the duty on steel in ingots, bars, sheets, and wire above a certain thickness is 2¼ cents, and that we had raised it to 3¼ cents, while reducing the duty a little on less important classes of steel. Let me state the case fairly. The present duty on ingots, bars, sheet, and wire not less than one quarter of an inch in diameter, valued at 7 cents per pound or less, is 2¼ cents per pound; value 7 and not above 11 cents per pound, 3 cents per pound; valued above 11 cents a pound, 3½ cents per pound and 10 per cent. *ad valorem.* The gentleman attempted to discredit the evidence which proves the magnitude of the frauds persistently perpetrated by the Sheffield steel makers for the last twenty years under this system; but the Secretary of the Treasury is acting upon it, and is largely increasing the revenues of the country from steel by requiring it to be honestly invoiced.

Much evidence, confirmed by the admission of one of the firms engaged in it, establish the fact that a combination has existed among these wealthy Englishmen to sell no steel in England to Americans, but send it to agents in this country for sale, and to so undervalue it that that which should pay 3½ cents and 10 per cent. *ad valorem* has, to the extent of 9 pounds out of every 10, been undervalued and brought in at 3 cents, and by the same fraudulent device and conspiracy the greater part of that which was subject to a duty of 3 cents has come in at 2¼.

Thus the Government has been defrauded of many millions of revenue. Now, what has the committee done in the premises? We have agreed to put all steel—that which was below and that which was above, that which paid 2¼ cents a pound and that which paid 5½ cents a pound, or 3½ cents and 10 per cent. *ad valorem*—under a duty of 3¼ cents per pound. We had steel importers and steel manufacturers and experts before us, and they all agreed that there was no conceivable test by which examiners and inspectors of customs could distinguish between steel worth from 4 to 7 cents and that worth more than 11 cents a pound; so that though we may thereby for a brief time do some injustice to those who use low-priced steel and those who produce high qualities of steel we have made a single duty, which will give us honest revenue and enable our steel manufacturers to live and extend their works.

In my recent remarks on Mr. Wells's report I quoted the language of the senior partner of a steel-making firm in Sheffield, England, in which he admitted the fact of undervaluation, and declared that while the law remains as it is the Government will be defrauded and cannot prevent it. Thus the honest men among the English steel-makers implore us to close the door against fraud in which they must participate, or surrender our market to their less honest neighbors. Yet, for our well-devised effort to do justice to the Government and honest importers, we are denounced as taxing the people to build up monopolies!

The gentleman from Iowa will I am sure pardon me for correcting a statement of his, on which he amplified somewhat to-day touching steel-manufacturing in Pittsburg. The statement he read yesterday was not that her steel-makers were able to compete with England in 1859; it was that steel-making in that city first became an assured success in that year. Her enterprising men of capital had for many years been renewing the yet fruitless experiment. Man after man and firm after firm had failed. Steel-works depreciated in value and new firms bought the stock and premises of old ones at reduced values, till, in 1859, "an assured success was attained." This was the phrase the gentleman from Iowa used yesterday when he had the paper before him.

STEPHEN COLWELL.

I am quite sure that he would not intentionally misstate a fact. Nobody values him more highly than I do. He is as earnest on his side of this great question as I am on mine, and we are both of a temperament that requires us to have the figures before us to prevent a certain measure of exaggeration in our statements. There is, however, one point on which I am disposed to quarrel with him, and that is that he should have assumed to have found an ally in my venerable friend, Stephen Colwell, and by a perversion of his language made him seem to plead against protection for American labor when the very words he quoted were written in its behalf. Sir, Stephen Colwell's life has been devoted to his country. It has been a life-long labor of love with him to promote the development of her vast stores of wealth and the prosperity of her farmers and laborers. He was the friend and companion of Frederick List, the founder of the German Zollverein, who was for a few years an exile from his native land and a dweller in the then undeveloped coal regions of Pennsylvania. After his death Mr. Colwell collected his writings and found pleasure in editing them; he has also written and published much in defense of protection as a sure means of promoting national greatness, cheap commodities, and the prosperity of the people; and I confess that I was both astonished and grieved that a portion of an article of Mr. Colwell's demanding the repeal of internal tax-

ation, and showing that it is a b[...] manufacturers and a burden [...] producers, should be quoted [...] from Iowa against the tariff [...] that protective duties add to [...] modities. I know my friend [...] the wrong he was doing, but [...] my venerable friend, whose [...] close, that his language shoul[...] before the nation whose int[...] much to promote.

THE CLASSIFICATION O[...]

But the gentleman fro[...] classification of iron fo[...] adopted by the committee. [...] Sir, so far as classification [...] ified, and the changes ar[...] the expressed opinion [...] former Committee of W[...]

The Senate of the Unit[...] of January, 1867, passed [...] 18th of February of that [...] of Ways and Means repo[...] with certain amendment[...] tee, finding a classification [...] ate and House, followed it[...] thought change necessary or [...] is the classification of whic[...] complains.

I am too weary, and too mu[...] and your patience is too fa[...] proceed further with the di[...] ent. There are points I wo[...] sider; but I must draw to a [...]

PROOF THAT PROTECTION C[...]

The gentleman from India[...] speaking of my argument on [...] said that as America produced [...] per annum, the establishment [...] could have had no influence up[...] English rails, because the quan[...] was relatively so small. I pr[...] trate the fallacy of that arg[...] tents of the little box I hold [...] long as America was unprepa[...] semer steel no Englishman would [...] rails for less than $150. I have [...] to this committee once, and I will [...] repeat the details. But when in 186[...] of Griswold & Co., at Troy, New Y[...] the Freedom Works, at Harrisburg[...] vania, were ready to deliver Besse[...] Englishman who had been swearing [...] could not sell them at less than [...] immediately offered them at $190. [...] our works increased from two to six [...] their price down to $100, and if [...] will drop it to $50, or until they [...] ers of our establishments to [...] duction and apply their premises and mac[...] to some other use.

Their policy is to crowd out our w[...] as Lord Brougham advised in 1815[...] the close of our war, "to spend any [...] money to strangle in the cradle the [...] dustries the exigencies of the war [...]

into existence in the United States." They spend any amount of money to crowd out five or six Bessemer-rail works, and then the price up to figures that will be satis to themselves.

and I would illustrate the argument by the [...] of a small box I hold in my hand. It [...] a [...] very small articles and speci [...] the [...]terial of which they are made. [...] of a kind that till quite lately [...]ively in Germany. They then [...] at from $6 to $12 per gross. [...] this afforded so grand [...] Bes[...] rails did at $150 gold per [...] events prove, it must have [...]nce the close of the war [...] the interior of Tennessee a [...]lc, [...]hich these are specimens, [...] pieces.] This is carried not [...] by our transportation com [...], giving business to our rail [...] between the heart of Tennessee [...]usetts. There Yankee ingenuity [...] talc into gas-tips which will not [...] as the Germans make, and for [...] had the monopoly of our market. [...]merican men have embarked a large [...] this enterprise, and employ many [...] Tennessee and Massachusetts. They [...] making these little gas-tips and creat [...]arket for western grain, and converting [...]ived laborers from Europe into well [...]rican workingmen.

[...]ect has their enterprise had on the [...] porcelain gas-tips? The German man [...], who could not sell these gas-tips for [...] $6 to $12 a gross, now suddenly drop [...] price and are flooding the market with [...] at $2 a gross. At this price they will soon destroy their Yankee rival and regain their old monopoly.

Now, are we wrong when we say that if anybody makes a profit out of us we prefer that it shall be those who feed on American wheat, wear American wool, and give good wages to American workmen? The little gas tip illustrates the truth that American compe tition cheapens foreign commodities quite as well as the weightier article of steel rails.

SILK POPLINS.

Cases of this kind are continually coming before us. Let me tell you of another from away up in the mountain counties of New York, at Schoharie. A quiet, unpretending citizen, seeing that there were a large number of unemployed girls in and about the village, made the experiment of manufacturing an arti cle in great demand for ladies' dresses, known as silk poplins. He equaled the foreign goods in quality, was underselling them, and to the extent of his capacity to produce was driving them out of the market, when by a change in the wool tariff the duty on his goods was unin tentionally reduced, and the foreigners have him at a disadvantage; and if we do not pass this bill, or give him other relief, he must

close his factory, lose the capital he has invested in it, and scatter the formerly idle girls he now employs at good wages.

These are the facts of the case. The wool bill, in order to let coarse woolen goods in at a low rate, provides that when they are over a certain number of ounces to the square yard they shall come in at 40 per cent. Poplins are in considerable part of silk; they are finer and more valuable than any heavy woolen goods, but the silk add to their weight, and it has been held that the duty on them has been re duced from 60 to 40 per cent. Unless the relief proposed in this bill be given, Mr. Barr is likely to be ruined and his factory closed.

TIN AND NICKEL.

The present law puts a duty of 15 per cent. on tin in pigs or bars. We produce no tin, though I believe they have recently discovered a bed of ore in California, and it is thought to exist in Missouri. I hope it does, and that it may soon be developed. We cannot make tin plates by reason of the duties on block tin and palm-oil. This bill of the committee proposes to put palm-oil, an African product, and block tin on the free list; so that we may begin the manufacture of sheet tin, for which we export annually $8,000,000 in gold.

While we have no well-ascertained deposits of tin ore the country abounds in deposits of nickel. Missouri, Kentucky, Virginia, Penn sylvania, New Jersey, and Connecticut have large deposits of it; yet when the law of 1861 was passed its manufacture had not been at tempted; and a duty of 15 per cent., the same as that on block tin, was put on nickel. Our bill proposes to enable the men of Missouri to work the vast deposits of mine La Motte; the men of Kentucky to work the large deposits in that State, and the people of Connecticut to establish nickel works in the immediate vicinity of their great factories of Britannia and other white-metal wares by putting the same rate of duty on nickel that we have on copper, zinc, lead, iron, and other metals.

THE EFFECT OF PROTECTING NICKEL.

Now let me show you what will be the effect of this measure. I hold in my hand a letter from Evans & Askin, the great nickel manufacturers of England. They tell us how they will punish us if we increase the tariff on nickel; and I hope you will join me in invoking their pun ishment. But let them speak for themselves, as they do in this letter. It reads thus:

BIRMINGHAM, *March* 18, 1868.

DEAR SIR: Although it is now some time since we had the pleasure of corresponding we hear from time to time of the progress you are making in the nickel trade in America, and we trust you find the business a remunerative and successful one.

We hear that attempts are being made to influence Congress to increase largely the import duties on refined nickel, and although perhaps we might at first regret that the duties should be raised, we are not quite sure it would not ultimately be to our ad vantage; for, if the duties are so raised as to render the import of nickel almost prohibitory we shall at once adopt measures to send out one of the junior members of our firm and erect a nickel refinery in the States. In fact from the large quantities of nickel and cobalt ores offered to us by mine La Motte, the Haley Smelting Company, and several others, we are almost disposed to do so at once, as we think it might answer our purpose better than forwarding the refined article from this country. We are not, of course, selfish enough to wish a monopoly of the nickel trade in America, but we hope and intend to have a share of it, either by shipment to or refining in the States.

Should we decide upon erecting works in your country may we reckon on any supply of ore from your mine, in addition to other sources?

We are, dear sir, yours, faithfully,

EVANS & ASKIN.

Mr. Joseph Wharton.

Let them come on with their skilled nickel-makers; let them bring their capital by millions; let them, if they can, bring 100,000 people to consume the grain of Missouri; and we will give them all welcome. By increasing the duty on nickel from 15 to 40 per cent. mine La Motte will thus become a great manufacturing center, and there will be a new market, not dependent on long lines of railroad or ocean transportation, for the grain and wool of the valley of the Mississippi.

Now, Mr. Chairman, in conclusion, I plead with the gentlemen of the committee to forget their sectional feelings, to put aside party strife, to remember that the glory and the power of their country depend on the prosperi ligence, and aspiring hopes of the people and their children. I beg th know they all love their country, to sta industries, and to aid the poor and o laborers of other lands to escape fr of "rye and potatoes" to a land of fr and liberal wages, in which the dai the family will be of wheat, mutton pork, with the vegetables and the fr the States of our broad and then assure perous country.

Finding that space permits it, I a following statement showing the rev lected each year from 1789 to 1868, th of dutiable imports and free goods annually, and the average rate of du ports annually. It was carefully pre appears as one of the appendices of annual report of the Special Commis the Revenue. It is very suggestive those who remember the financial co the country from 1837 to 1842, and fr to 1861, the price of grain and the endured by the laboring people at all cial or manufacturing centers will pr clusive on many points:

The tariffs of the United States.

Dates.	Tariffs.	Customs.	Imports.		
			Free.	Dutiable.	Total.
From March 4, 1789, to Dec. 31,					
1790—August 10...	General		-		$52,200,000
1791—March 3....	Spirits	$4,399,473 09	-		31,500,000
1792—May 2........	General	3,443,070 85	-		31,100,000
1793		4,255,306 56	-		31,600,000
1794—June 7......	General	4,801,065 28	-		69,756,258
1795—January 29.	Supplementary	5,588,461 26	-		81,436,164
1796		6,567,987 94	-		75,379,406
1797—March 3......	General	7,549,649 65	-		68,551,700
1798		7,106,061 93	-		79,069,148
1799		6,610,449 31	-		91,252,768
1800—March 13....	Sugar and wines......	9,080,932 73	-		111,363,511
1801		10,750,778 93	-		76,333,333
1802		12,458,235 74	-		64,666,666
1803		10,479,417 61	-		85,000,000
1804—March 26....	Mediterranean fund.	11,098,565 33	-		120,000,000
1805—March 27....	Light money......	12,936,487 04	-		129,410,000
1806		14,667,698 17	-		138,500,000
1807		15,845,521 61	-		58,500,000
1808		16,363,550 58	-		59,400,000
1809		7,296,020 58	-		85,400,000
1810		8,583,309 31	-		53,400,000
1811		13,313,222 73	-		77,030,000
1812—July 1......	War, double duties..	8,958,777 53	-		22,005,000
1813—July 13........	Salt......	13,224,623 25	-		12,965,000
1814		5,998,772 08	-		13,041,274
1815		7,232,942 22	-		117,163,000
1816—April 27....	Min. for protection.	36,306,874 88	-		99,250,000
1817		26,283,348 49	-		121,750,000
1818—April 20....	Iron and alum........	17,176,385 90	-		87,125,000
1819—March 3.....	Wines........	20,283,608 76	-		74,450,000
1820		15,905,612 15	-		62,585,724
1821		18,475,703 57	$10,082,313	$52,503,411	83,241,541
1822		21,666,065 43	7,293,708	75,942,833	77,579,267
1823		22,402,634 29	9,048,288	68,530,979	80,549,007
1824—May 22.....	General rise........	25,486,817 86	12,563,773	67,985,234	96,340,075
1825		31,653,871 50	10,947,510	85,392,565	84,974,477
1826		26,053,861 97	12,567,769	72,466,798	

The tariffs of the United States—Continued.

Dates.	Tariffs.	Customs.	Imports.			Per cent. on dutiable.	Per cent. on aggregate.
			Free.	Dutiable.	Total.		
1827		27,948,956 57	11,855,104	67,628,964	79,484,068	41.3	35.1
1828—May 19	Min. extended	29,951,251 90	12,379,176	76,130,648	88,509,824	39.3	33.8
1829		27,688,701 11	11,805,501	62,687,026	74,492,527	44.3	37.1
1830—May 20	Coffee, tea, molasses.	28,389,505 05	12,746,245	58,130,675	70,876,920	48.8	40
1831		36,596,118 19	13,456,625	89,734,499	103,191,124	40.8	35.4
1832—July 14	Modifications	29,341,175 65	14,249,453	86,779,813	101,029,266	33.8	29
1833—March 2	Compromise	24,177,578 52	32,447,950	75,670,361	108,118,311	31.9	22.4
1834		18,960,705 96	68,393,180	58,128,152	125,521,332	22.6	15
1835		25,890,726 66	77,940,493	71,955,249	149,805,742	26.0	17.2
1836		30,818,327 67	92,056,481	97,923,554	189,980,035	31.6	16.2
1837		18,134,131 01	69,250,031	71,739,186	140,989,217	25.3	12.4
1838		19,702,825 45	60,860,005	52,857,399	113,717,404	37.8	17.3
1839		25,554,533 96	76,401,792	85,690,340	162,092,132	29.9	15.8
1840		15,104,790 63	57,196,204	49,945,315	107,141,519	30.4	14.1
1841—Sept. 11	Free list tax	19,919,492 17	66,019,731	61,926,446	127,946,177	32.2	15.6
1842—August 30	General rise	16,662,746 84	30,627,486	69,534,601	100,162,087	23.1	16.6
1843		10,208,000 43	35,574,584	29,179,215	64,753,799	35.7	15.7
1844		29,236,357 38	24,766,881	83,668,154	108,435,035	35.1	26.9
1845		30,952,416 21	22,147,840	95,106,724	117,254,564	32.5	26.4
1846—August 6	Revenue tariff	26,712,668 00	24,767,730	96,924,053	121,691,797	26½	21.9
1847		23,747,865 00	41,772,636	104,773,002	146,515,638	22½	16.2
1848		31,757,071 00	22,716,603	132,282,325	154,998,928	24	20.4
1849		28,346,739 00	22,377,665	125,479,774	147,857,439	23	19.2
1850		39,668,686 00	22,710,382	155,427,936	178,138,318	25.2	22.3
1851		49,017,568 00	25,106,587	191,118,345	216,224,932	26	22.6
1852		47,339,326 00	29,692,934	183,252,508	212,945,442	26	22.2
1853		58,931,865 00	31,383,534	236,595,113	267,978,647	25	22
1854		61,224,190 00	33,285,821	271,276,560	304,562,381	23.5	21.1
1855		53,025,794 00	40,090,336	221,378,184	261,468,520	23	20.3
1856		64,022,863 00	56,955,706	257,684,236	314,639,942	25	20.3
1857—March 3	General	63,875,905 00	66,729,306	294,160,835	360,890,141	21.5	17.7
1858		41,789,621 00	80,319,275	202,293,875	282,613,150	20	14.8
1859		49,565,824 00	79,721,116	259,017,014	338,708,130	19	14.6
1860		53,187,511 00	90,841,749	279,872,327	362,166,254	19	14.7
1861 {March 2 / August 5 / Dec. 24}		39,582,186 00	*134,550,196	218,180,191	352,739,387	18.1	11.2
1862—July 14	General	49,056,398 00	*91,603,491	183,843,458	275,446,939	26.7	17.7
1863—March 3		69,059,642 00	44,826,629	208,093,891	252,919,920	33.2	23.7
1864—June 30	General	102,316,153 00	*54,244,183	275,320,951	329,565,134	37.2	31
1865—March 3		84,928,260 00	54,329,588	194,226,064	248,555,652	43.7	34.2
1866 {March 14 / May 16 / July 28}		179,046,630 00	69,728,618	375,783,540	445,512,158	47.06	40.2
1867—March 2	Wool and woolens	176,417,811 00	39,105,708	372,627,601	411,733,309	47.34	42.8
1868		164,464,599 55	29,804,147	343,605,301	373,409,448	47.86	44
1869—Feb. 24	Copper increased	180,048,426 63	41,179,172	395,847,369	437,026,541	45.48	41.2

* In these amounts are included imports into the southern ports during the war, from which no revenue was derived, namely, in 1861, $17,089,234; in 1862, $90,789, and in 1864, $2,220.

CPSIA information can be obtained
at www.ICGtesting.com
Printed in the USA
BVHW071416090119
537429BV00013B/1316/P